Authorship and Identity in Late Thirteenth-Century Motets

Questions of authorship are central to the late thirteenth-century motet repertoire represented by the seventh section or fascicle of the Montpellier Codex (Montpellier, Bibliothèque interuniversitaire, Section de médecine, H. 196, hereafter **Mo**). **Mo** does not explicitly attribute any of its compositions, but theoretical sources name Petrus de Cruce as the composer of the two motets that open fascicle 7, and three later motets in this fascicle are elsewhere ascribed to Adam de la Halle. This monograph reveals a musical and textual quotation of Adam's *Aucun se sont loe* incipit at the outset of Petrus's *Aucun ont trouve* triplum, and it explores various invocations of Adam and Petrus – their works and techniques – within further anonymous compositions. Authorship is additionally considered from the perspective of two new types of motets especially prevalent in fascicle 7: motets that name musicians, as well as those based on vernacular song or instrumental melodies, some of which are identified by the names of their creators. This book offers new insights into the musical, poetic, and curatorial reception of thirteenth-century composers' works in their own time. It uncovers, beneath the surface of an anonymous motet book, unsuspected interactions between authors and traces of compositional identities.

Catherine A. Bradley is Professor at the University of Oslo.

Royal Musical Association Monographs
Series Editor: Simon P. Keefe

This series was originally supported by funds made available to the Royal Musical Association from the estate of Thurston Dart, former King Edward Professor of Music at the University of London. The editorial board is the Publications Committee of the Association.

No.34: The Pre-History of The Midsummer Marriage Narratives and Speculations: Narratives and Speculations
Roger Savage

No.35: Felice Giardini and Professional Music Culture in mid-eighteenth-century London
Cheryll Duncan

No.36: Disinformation in Mass Media: Gluck, Piccinni and the Journal de Paris
Beverly Jerold

No.37: Music Theory in Late Medieval Avignon: Music Theory in Late Medieval Avignon
Karen M. Cook

No. 38: Gregorio Ballabene's Forty-eight-part Mass for Twelve Choirs (1772)
Florian Bassani

No. 39: Authorship and Identity in Late Thirteenth-Century Motets
Catherine A. Bradley

For more information about this series, please visit: www.routledge.com/music/series/RMA

Authorship and Identity in Late Thirteenth-Century Motets

Catherine A. Bradley

Routledge
Taylor & Francis Group
LONDON AND NEW YORK

First published 2022
by Routledge
4 Park Square, Milton Park, Abingdon, Oxon OX14 4RN

and by Routledge
605 Third Avenue, New York, NY 10158

Routledge is an imprint of the Taylor & Francis Group, an informa business

British Library Cataloguing-in-Publication Data
A catalogue record for this book is available from the British Library

Library of Congress Cataloging-in-Publication Data
A catalog record for this book has been requested

ISBN: 978-1-032-19457-8 (hbk)
ISBN: 978-1-032-19460-8 (pbk)
ISBN: 978-1-003-25928-2 (ebk)

DOI: 10.4324/9781003259282

Typeset in Times New Roman
by Apex CoVantage, LLC

Contents

Tables

Music Examples

Acknowledgements

First and foremost, I thank Lawrence Earp for the insight and care with which he painstakingly read and commented on this book. He kindly provided expert guidance at various points throughout the process and his many fruitful and constructive suggestions have improved the material immeasurably.

I am especially indebted to Margaret Bent, Elizabeth Eva Leach, and David Maw, all of whom read and discussed with me drafts of the entire manuscript and who were characteristically generous in offering invaluable feedback.

This project began during a Wigeland Research and Teaching Fellowship at the University of Chicago in early 2020. I owe this wonderful opportunity to Anne Walters Robertson, and I thank her and Martha Feldman for their unstinting hospitality. I am grateful to the Department of Music, at which I was privileged to offer a PhD seminar on medieval motets, benefiting enormously from the insights and inspiration of Patrick Dittamo, Natalie Farrell, and Jacob Reed.

I profited hugely from the chance to discuss Chapter 2 with the Yale University Medieval Song Lab in 2020, for which I thank Anna Zayaruznaya and Ardis Butterfield.

I thank Simon Keefe and Heidi Bishop at RMA monographs for handling the publication process with efficiency and humanity. I am indebted to Bonnie Blackburn for copy-editing and indexing the manuscript with such skill.

I warmly thank friends, colleagues, and mentors at the University of Oslo and around the world for their input and encouragement, especially Karen Desmond, Gaël Saint-Cricq, and – as ever – Susan Rankin.

This book was funded by a European Research Council (ERC) Consolidator Grant under the European Union Horizon 2020 research and innovation program (Grant number 864174) in the context of the project *BENEDICAMUS: Musical and Poetic Creativity for a Unique Moment in the Western Christian Liturgy c.1000–1500.*

Manuscript Sigla and Abbreviations

Manuscript Sigla

Add. 24198	London, British Library, Add. 24198
Add. 41667	London, British Library, Add. 41667(I)
Amiens	Amiens, Bibliothèque municipale, 126
Arras frag.	Lost (copy in private collection viewed and catalogued by Friedrich Ludwig in 1906)
ArsA	Paris, Bibliothèque de l'Arsenal, 135
ArsC	Paris, Bibliothèque de l'Arsenal, 8521
Ba	Bamberg, Staatsbibliothek, Lit. 115 (formerly Ed.IV.6)
Bes	Besançon, Bibliothèque municipale, I, 716
Ca	Cambrai, Le Labo (formerly Bibliothèque municipale), A 410 (formerly 386)
CaB	Cambrai, Le Labo (formerly Bibliothèque municipale), B 1328
CgC	Cambridge, Gonville and Caius College, 11/11
Cl	Paris, Bibliothèque nationale de France, NAF 13521, 'La Clayette'
Da	Darmstadt, Hessische Landes- und Hochschulbibliothek, 3471
Dijon 447	Dijon, Bibliothèque municipale, 447
Dijon 526	Dijon, Bibliothèque municipale, 526
Douce 139	Oxford, Bodleian Library, Douce 139
Douce 308	Oxford, Bodleian Library, Douce 308
DRc 20	Durham, Cathedral Library, C. I. 20
F	Florence, Biblioteca Medicea Laurenziana, Plut. 29.1
F 122	Florence, Biblioteca Nazionale Centrale, Banco Rari 18
F 212	Florence, Biblioteca Nazionale Centrale, Banco Rari 19
Fauv	Paris, Bibliothèque nationale de France, Fr. 146, 'Interpolated Roman de Fauvel'
Fr. 1569	Paris, Bibliothèque nationale de France, Fr. 1569
Fr. 14968	Paris, Bibliothèque nationale de France, Fr. 14968
Ha	Paris, Bibliothèque nationale de France, Fr. 25566 (contains Adam de la Halle *opera omnia*)
Hu	Burgos, Monasterio de Las Huelgas, 11 (formerly IX)

Ivrea	Ivrea, Biblioteca capitolare, 115
Lat. 15131	Paris, Bibliothèque nationale de France, Lat. 15131
Leuven	Leuven, Collection Gilbert Huybens, D
Lille	Lille, Bibliothèque municipale, 316
LoB	London, British Library, Egerton 274
LoD	London, British Library, Add. 27630
Méjanes	Aix-en-Provence, Bibliothèque Méjanes, 166
Mo	Montpellier, Bibliothèque interuniversitaire, Section de médecine, H. 196
MuC	Munich, Bayerische Staatsbibliothek, Clm. 5539
N	Paris, Bibliothèque nationale de France, Fr. 12615, 'Noailles chansonnier'
Ob 7	Oxford, Bodleian Library, e Mus. 7
Ob E 42	Oxford, Bodleian Library, Lat. liturg. e 42
Onc	Oxford, New College Library, 362
PaB	Paris, Bibliothèque nationale de France, Fr. 12786
PsAr	Paris, Bibliothèque nationale de France, Lat. 11266
Reg	Rome, Biblioteca Apostolica Vaticana, Reg. lat. 1543 (fragments)
Renart C	Paris, Bibliothèque nationale de France, Fr. 372
Renart F	Paris, Bibliothèque nationale de France, Fr. 1593
Renart L	Paris, Bibliothèque nationale de France, Fr. 1581
StM	Saint-Maurice, Abbey of Saint-Maurice-en-Valais, 4
Stockholm	Stockholm, Riksarkivet, Fragment 813
StV	Paris, Bibliothèque nationale de France, Lat. 15139
Tours	Tours, Bibliothèque municipale, 925
Trémoïlle	Paris, Bibliothèque nationale de France, NAF 23190
Trier	Trier, Stadtbibliothek, 322/1994
Trouv. K	Paris, Bibliothèque de l'Arsenal, 5198
Trouv. N	Paris, Bibliothèque nationale de France, Fr. 845
Trouv. O	Paris, Bibliothèque nationale de France, Fr. 846
Trouv. P	Paris, Bibliothèque nationale de France, Fr. 847
Trouv. R	Paris, Bibliothèque nationale de France, Fr. 1591
Trouv. U	Paris, Bibliothèque nationale de France, Fr. 20050
Trouv. V	Paris, Bibliothèque nationale de France, Fr. 25506
Trouv. X	Paris, Bibliothèque nationale de France, NAF 1050
Tu	Turin, Biblioteca Reale, varia 42
Udine	Udine, Biblioteca Comunale Vincenzo Joppi, 290
Vat	Rome, Biblioteca Apostolica Vaticana, Reg. lat. 1490
Vorau	Vorau, Bibliothek des Augustiner Chorherrenstifts, 23 (Fragment 118D)
W2	Wolfenbüttel, Herzog August Bibliothek, Cod. Guelf. 1099 Helmst. (Heinemann no. 1206)
Wilh	Wilhering, Stiftsbibliothek IX 40

Abbreviations

Add.   Additional
Fr.   Français
Lat.   Latin
NAF   Nouvelles acquisitions françaises
Reg.   Regina
RS   Song number in Raynaud-Spanke 1980
SB   Semibreve
vdB   Refrain number in van den Boogaard 1969

A Note on Transcriptions

Original text spellings are retained within transcriptions of a particular manuscript source but general references to motets or refrains follow the standardised titles established in Gennrich 1957 and van den Boogaard 1969 respectively. Capitalisation, punctuation, and text-line numbers are editorial.

Square brackets indicate editorial insertions.

Ligatures are indicated by square brackets, and conjuncturae by dashed slurs. Plicae are shown by a line through the stem.

Unless otherwise indicated, the medieval note value of a perfect or ternary long (*longa*) is equivalent to a dotted minim in modern notation. This is the unit of the 'perfection', by which musical time is measured throughout.

The interpretation of semibreves reflects the ternary conception of the breve espoused by Lambertus and Franco. Pairs of semibreves are therefore unequal and the first of the pair is interpreted as the shorter, minor or *recta*, semibreve (in parallel with the practice for breves). I maintain the overall tripartite conception of the breve where this unit contains four or more semibreves: in the absence of any clear medieval theoretical prescription, I adopt the fast-notes-first principle (typically applied to conjuncturae).

Contents of Montpellier Codex Fascicle 7

Latin motet texts are highlighted in bold to allow quick identification of Latin and bilingual motets. Motet numbers and Mass/Office plainchant numbers, after Gennrich 1957, are given in square brackets. For concordances, '&' differentiates a concordance in a different version, with reduced voices and/or contrafactum text(s).

No.	Folio[1]	Gathering	Triplum	Motetus	Tenor	Concordances
253	270r–273r	I	S'amours eust point de poer [531a]	Au renouveler du joli tans [531b]	ECCE [IAM] [M 61]	**Tu**
254	273r–275r		Aucun ont trouve chant [106]	Lonc tens me sui tenu [107]	ANNUN[TIANTES] [M 9]	**Tu**
255	275r–277v		J'ai mis toute ma pensee [609]	Je n'en puis mais, se je ne chant [610]	PUERORUM [M 86b, KYRIE]	**Bes, Tu** & **Ca** (2vv), **Douce 308** (motetus text)
256	277v–279r	II (begins fol. 278r)	Entre Copin et Bourgois [866]	Je me cuidoie tenir [867]	BELE YSABELOS	**Ba, Bes, Tu**
257	279r–280v		Plus joliement c'onques mais [292]	Quant li douz tans se debrise [293]	PORTARE [M 22]	**Tu** & **Ob E 42** (Latin contrafacta)
258	280v–282r		Entre Adan et Haniket [725]	Chief bien seantz [726]	APTATUR [O 46]	**Ba, Bes, Ha, Tu, Vorau,**
259	282r–283v		Par un matinet l'autrier m'aloie [295]	Les un bosket vi Robechon [296]	PORTARE [M 22]	**Ba, Bes**
260	283v–284v		Au cuer, ai un mal [868]	Ja ne m'en repentirai d'amer [869]	JOLIETEMENT &c	**Ba, Bes, Tu, Douce 139**

(Continued)

(Continued)

No.	Folios	Section				
290	330r–332r		Nouvele amour m'a saisi [882]	Haute amor m'a assalli [883]	HE DAME JOLIE MON CUER &c	—
291	332r–333v		Bien met amours son pooir [884]	Dame, alegies ma grevance [885]	A PARIS [*sic*] [APERIS, M 69]	**Bes**
First supplement						
292	333v–335r	IX (begins fol. 334r)	De chanter me vient talens [860]	Bien doi boine amor loer [861]	CHOSE TASSIN [B]	—
293	335r–336v		Donne ma dame ai mon cuer [620]	Adies sont ces sades brunetes [621]	KYRIE CELUM [M 86f]	—
294	336v–338r		Entre Jehan et Philippet [862]	Nus hom ne puet desiervir [863]	CHOSE TASSIN [C]	—
295	338r–339r		Toutes voies m'a amours assailli [886]	Trop ai de griete pour [887]	JE LA TRUIS TROP ASPRETE &c	—
296	339r–v		Boine amours mi me fait chanter [299]	Uns maus savereus et dous [300]	PORTARE [M 22]	—
297	339v–341v		Quant che vient en mai [864]	Mout ai este longement [865]	CHOSE LOYSET	—
298	341v–344r	X (begins fol. 342r)	Lonc tans ai atendu le mierchi [571]	Tant ai souffert en amant [572]	SURREXIT [M 75]	—

(Continued)

No.	Folio[1]	Gathering	Triplum	Motetus	Tenor	Concordances
299	344r–345v		Pour chou que j'aim ma dame [622]	Li jolis tans, que je voi revenir [623]	KYRIELEISON [M 86g]	–
Second supplement						
300	346r–v		**Salve, virgo virginum, salve, sancta parens** [36]	**Salve, sancta parens** [36]	OMNES [M 1]	–
301	347r–348r		–	**Laqueus conteritur venantium** [95]	LAQUEUS [M 7]	**LoB**
302	348r–349v		**Theotheca, virgo geratica** [878]	Las, pour qoi l'eslonge tant [879]	QUI PRANDROIT &c (= no. 277)	–

1 This foliation follows the manuscript's original inked foliation (top centre) rather than the pencil foliation at top right (used in Tischler 1978). Owing to the loss of the bifolio 303/308, the pencil foliation is two integers behind from its folio 307r (ink fol. 309r) on. The centred ink foliation changes from Roman to Arabic numerals on its fol. 334r, at the start of the first supplement.

Introduction

Anonymity reigns, outwardly at least, within thirteenth-century motet collections where pieces are never accompanied by author ascriptions. Definite information about motet creators is therefore limited, gleaned only from external contexts. Medieval documents or theoretical treatises sometimes name motet composers, and motet material occasionally appears within different types of music and/or text sources in which author ascriptions are conventional. Fortuitously and unusually, such information exists to reveal the respective identities of two motet composers in the concluding sections of the Montpellier Codex, the thirteenth century's largest and most lavish motet collection (Montpellier, Bibliothèque interuniversitaire, Section de médecine, H. 196, hereafter **Mo**). The first two motets of **Mo**'s seventh section or fascicle are attributed in later theoretical treatises to Petrus de Cruce, who is associated with a style of multi-semibreve text declamation evident in several further compositions in the codex. Adam de la Halle is known to be the composer of three motets in fascicle 7, since they appear in a section of the manuscript Paris, Bibliothèque nationale de France, Fr. 25566 (hereafter **Ha**) that records what is apparently an *opera omnia*: original rubrics explicitly name Adam as the creator of monophonic songs and dramatic and poetic works, as well as of groups of polyphonic rondeaux and motets.

These motet attributions to Petrus and to Adam are very well known, long recognised and emphasised in discussions of a polyphonic repertoire that is otherwise devoid of composer figures. There seems to have been an initial tendency cautiously to extend the reach of these known personalities as far as possible. As discussed in Chapter 4, scholars have posited that some or all of the motets in the multi-note style associated with Petrus might be by him (not just the two quoted and attributed by theorists).[1] And five anonymous

---

1 See the six possible additional works by Petrus suggested by Ernest H. Sanders and Peter
   M. Lefferts in 'Petrus de Cruce', *Grove Music Online* (accessed 15 Aug. 2020) https://

DOI: 10.4324/9781003259282-1

motets in **Mo** fascicle 7 that employ refrains from rondeaux attributed to Adam in **Ha**, but which are not themselves present in this *opera omnia*, were tentatively suggested as his creations.[2] More recently, however, scholars have adopted an increasingly judicious and critical stance. Far from attributing all multi-note compositions in **Mo** to Petrus, Margaret Bent has also challenged the established use of the term 'Petronian' for motets that subdivide perfect breves into more than three semibreves, emphasising evidence from the fourteenth-century theorist Jacobus, which suggests that Petrus was neither the true innovator nor the most radical proponent of the style that is typically named after him.[3] In the case of Adam de la Halle, Mark Everist's suggestion that it is 'perhaps more likely, and easier to prove' that Adam was familiar with the repertoire of **Mo** fascicle 7, than that the composers of other motets in **Mo** 7 knew Adam's rondeaux, remains largely accepted.[4] This renders the five anonymous motets in **Mo** 7 that contain rondeau refrains linked to Adam not as works by him or quoting him but rather as sources on which Adam later drew. Everist's 2018 survey of **Mo**'s eighth fascicle underlines the fact that, under the broadest possible definition, 'Petronian' motets make up only around 10 per cent of the total repertoire of **Mo** 7 and 8.[5] Everist draws attention to other and lesser-known motet typologies in these fascicles, which are explored in detail in Chapters 3 and 5.[6] He suggests that groups of related pieces of a particular provenance or on a particular type of tenor quotation in fascicles 7 and 8 may be of greater significance than those by or associated with Petrus or Adam.[7]

These interventions have laid the ground for a profitable and nuanced return to questions of authorship and compositional identity, where the use of certain types of short notes or refrains is not simply reduced to an

---

doi.org/10.1093/gmo/9781561592630.article.21491. Tischler 1978 includes these tentative attributions to Petrus (with the exception of **Mo** 7, no. 298). Crocker 1990, 670 n. 50, delineates a slightly different group of works similar to those known to by Petrus, while Maw 2018 (see esp. 164, Table 9.1) considers all of the motets in **Mo** 7 and 8 that divide their breves into four or more semibreves to be by Petrus.

2   See Robert Falck, 'Adam de la Halle', *Grove Music Online* (accessed 27 Mar. 2020), https://doi.org/10.1093/gmo/9781561592630.article.00163. Falck and the edition of Adam's lyric works in Wilkins 1967 also include in the category of uncertain or possible works by Adam a further anonymous motet in fascicle 8 (**Mo** 8, no. 316), which quotes the incipit of a motetus by Adam.

3   Bent 2015, 39–43, discussed in detail in Chapter 4.

4   Everist 1996, 88–89, reprinted in Everist 2019, 329.

5   Everist 2018, 20–21.

6   These are the 'English' motets' (Everist 2018, 21–24), which are more prevalent in fascicle 8 and are not discussed here; the 'confraternity motets' naming musicians (24–48) that are the focus of Chapter 3; and the 'Tassin and Loyset' motets (28–29) and 'song-tenor' motets (29–30) examined in Chapter 5.

7   Everist 2018, 29.

attribution and considered only to this end. This is the aim of the present monograph, which explores instead the extent to which anonymous works in **Mo** fascicles 7 and 8 themselves represent engagement with or invocation of particular composer figures and their techniques, considering the forms which such engagement can take, and what such engagement reveals about the status of the composers in question as well as the musical cultures within which they operated. This approach offers new insights into the musical, poetic, and curatorial reception of thirteenth-century composers' works in their own time, uncovering traces of compositional personalities and interactions between composers otherwise lost to posterity.

There exists frustratingly little hard evidence about the lives of either Adam or Petrus. As discussed in Chapter 2, we do not know birth or death dates for either of them nor, with certainty, their respective generations, but it seems that Adam may have been dead by 1290, while Petrus was alive and well in Amiens around 1300. Dating of manuscript sources and theoretical treatises in this period is also conjectural, relative, and debated: Franco of Cologne's *Ars cantus mensurabilis musicae* presumably pre-dates Petrus's more radical motets, and is in turn pre-dated by Johannes de Garlandia's *De mensurabili musica*, on which it draws. Petrus himself is strongly identified with fascicle 7 of **Mo** – the first extant source to contain his compositions – such that his heyday and **Mo** 7's copying have long been aligned. This monograph works with presumed datings but does not take them for granted, interrogating the evidence on which they are based. Although such interrogation does not substantially alter received views, the chapters that follow piece together a new body of circumstantial and contextual evidence, which serves independently to confirm that current relative and accepted datings for manuscripts, motets, and theoretical treatises in the late thirteenth century are broadly realistic.

The date of Adam's complete works compilation – whose literary texts contain some helpful datable clues – has not been given serious consideration in relation to **Mo** fascicle 7, in which Adam also plays an important role. Adam's *opera omnia* is the first of several sections in the compendium manuscript **Ha**. It is preceded here by an independent gathering of noticeably different size and appearance, which was later inserted into **Ha** (now occupying fols. 2r–9v) and records fourteen of Adam's *grands chants*, all of which are already present in the following *opera omnia*. **Ha** contains three sumptuous full-page miniatures that may also have been subsequent additions, but otherwise the manuscript was, as Alison Stones recently observed, 'most likely conceived and produced as a whole'.[8] Certain events referenced in literary texts in **Ha** are important as regards its date: Adam's

---

8 Stones 2019, 88. On artistic grounds, Stones 2019, 87, dates **Ha**'s full-page miniatures c.1300, suggesting (at 88) that they may have been created in a 'second phase of production'.

own *Le Roi de Sezile* declares that it was interrupted by the death of Charles of Anjou in 1285. Beyond Adam's section of the manuscript, the copy of Jacquemart Gielee's *Renart le nouvel* preserves a colophon dated 1289 (fol. 176v). John Haines has demonstrated conclusively that the year of composition declared in one other of the four extant *Renart le nouvel* colophons must be too early, suggesting that this applies also in **Ha**, and placing the date of completion of *Renart le nouvel* in its current forms around 1291 or 1292.[9] This is in keeping with another text in **Ha**, the *Dis dou vrai Aniel*, that makes reference to the city of Acre, which fell from Christian power in May 1291. This year has been cited both as a *terminus post* and *ante quem* for the date of the *Dis*; however, as Adolf Tobler noted, it is not quite clear from the narrative whether Acre has actually fallen yet or not.[10] In either case, though, it seems probable that the *Dis dou vrai Aniel* dates from the early 1290s when this event was reasonably current. Carol Symes considers the Adam compilation in **Ha** to be a 'memorial anthology' of his works commissioned 'towards the end of the 1280s'.[11] This remains plausible within the context of textual references to external events in **Ha** overall, which place Adam's *opera omnia* definitely after 1285, with a probable date for the compendium as a whole in the early 1290s.

This dating for **Ha** accords with that conventionally accepted for **Mo** fascicle 7, the section of the anonymous motet book that records three of Adam's five known motets. The compilation of **Mo** still presents something of a conundrum, both chronologically and conceptually, since the codex encompasses several layers of additions both beyond and within its final fascicles.[12]

---

9   Haines 2010, 25–34, esp. 34. The colophon in **Renart L** is dated 1288, but its text contains a section that makes reference to the fall of Acre, which did not occur until 1291. This section with the reference to Acre is, however, absent from **Ha**, and nothing within this copy of the *Renart* text can prove that the 1289 date in its colophon is incorrect. In the case of **Ha**, it therefore remains possible that the scribe was copying literally from an exemplar whose text genuinely had been completed in 1289.

10 Everist 1996, 59 n. 2; Ibos-Augé 2018b, 233, have taken 1291 to be a *terminus post quem*. By contrast, Shagrir 2019, 76–77, states that the *Dis dou vrai Aniel* describes a time when the Christian control of Acre was still under threat, that is, before its fall in 1291. Shagrir 2019, 77 n. 2, cites Tobler 1884 in support of this argument. In fact, Tobler ultimately concluded (at xix) that 'it must remain undecided whether our poem was compiled before or after 1291' ('So muss denn wohl unentschieden gelassen werden, ob unsere Dichtung vor oder nach 1291 abgefasst ist').

11 Symes 2019, 22; Huot 1987a, 64, dated the manuscript 'in the late thirteenth century'. Stones's slightly later dating of the illustrations c.1300 (see n. 8) could confirm that they are indeed later additions to the manuscript. The dating of 'between 1291 and 1297' in Everist 1996, 59 n. 2, relies on the *Dis dou vrai Aniel* as a *terminus post quem* and details of heraldry in the, possibly later, full-page miniatures for the *terminus ante quem*.

12 Accepted datings for **Mo** fascicles 1–7 are those advanced in Everist 1989, 110–34, which rely in large part on art-historical evidence from Branner 1977. For a summary of the various positions and debates on the dating of **Mo**'s 'old corpus' and fascicle 7, see Parsoneault 2001, 130–52.

Fascicles 1 and 7 are thought to have been added to surround the so-called old corpus (fascicles 2–6, dated c.1270) at the same time. The addition of these outer fascicles is dated c.1290, at which same moment several motets were also added on empty folios at the end of fascicles 3 and 5, and a table of contents was then created for **Mo**'s seven fascicles. Yet fascicle 7 itself contains two distinct 'supplements' (each marked by a change of scribe and of ink) that were subsequently appended to the thirty-nine motets in the fascicle proper: these supplements do not bear the inked and centred Roman folio numbers of the earlier part of the codex, and their motets are absent from **Mo**'s medieval table of contents.[13] Only seven out of the thirty-nine motets in the main body of fascicle 7 are unica, but the first supplement presents a wholly unique group of eight French three-voice motets, while two of the second supplement's three pieces (two Latin motets and a bilingual motet) are also unique. Although **Mo**'s table of contents confirms a definite disjunction, Alison Stones has concluded that the whole of fascicle 7 was decorated by a single artist, and the two supplements are typically encompassed within the rough 1290s dating.[14] The fascicle's decorative continuity would seem to indicate that its three internal layers were not too chronologically disparate.

The status of **Mo** fascicle 8, decorated by a different artist from that of fascicle 7, adds an additional layer of chronological complication.[15] On the one hand, Sean Curran's scrutiny of fascicle 8's text hand places it relative in proximity to fascicle 7, between around 1290 and 1310.[16] On the other, analyses by Rebecca A. Baltzer and Stones of the decoration of **Mo** 8 point, respectively, to the 1310s or even as late as 1325.[17] Fascicle 8, then, was surely a later creation than fascicle 7 – though exactly how much later remains in doubt – and a somewhat separate one since, as Baltzer observed, its decorations were on a slightly smaller scale to the rest of the manuscript.[18] Nevertheless, the historiated initial for **Mo** 8's opening *Deus in adiutorium* (fol. 350r) is undoubtedly a direct nod to the similarly decorated *Deus in adiutorium* at the start of fascicle 1 (fol. 1r). It seems, therefore, that fascicle 8 simultaneously had the status of a self-contained collection and one that was connected to and responded to the rest of **Mo**.[19]

This book takes as its focus the body of motets recorded, often uniquely, in **Mo** fascicle 7 and its supplements, as well as the additional collection in

---

13 The different scribal hands and layers of **Mo** 7 were first outlined in Ludwig 1978, 425–26. See also Wolinski 1992, 265–75.

14 Stones 2018, 75, n. 14.

15 Ibid., 75.

16 Curran 2018, 41.

17 See Baltzer 2018, 88; Stones 2018, 77. Baltzer proposed a date of decoration in the (early) thirteen-teens, while Stones suggests a date of c.1315–25.

18 Baltzer 2018, 78.

19 On fascicle 8's position with respect to **Mo** as a whole, see Bradley and Desmond 2018, 6.

fascicle 8. Chapter 1 seeks to demonstrate that all of the motets in **Mo** 7 and 8 known to contain materials linked to Adam de la Halle do so under the banner of quotations, some of which are self-quotations. It argues for the significance of Adam's author status within the context of these anonymous motet fascicles, proposing – in Chapter 2 – a previously unnoticed quotation of Adam by Petrus de Cruce, whose famous triplum *Aucun ont trouve* opens with a musical and textual reference to Adam's triplum *Aucun se sont loe*. An increased sense of Adam's presence and influence in the late thirteenth-century motet repertoire at large, and the possibility of a direct link between Adam and Petrus – composers from Arras and Amiens, respectively – opens up questions of chronology, biography, and geography, as well as of author personalities and interrelationships within the compositional milieu as recorded in the Parisian manuscript **Mo**. More generally, these kinds of interrelationships are explicitly documented in the group of works that is the focus of Chapter 3: motets, one of which is attributed to Adam, that themselves name and describe the activities of communities of musicians.

Chapter 4 shifts the focus away from Adam towards Petrus, the composer whose two known works open the collection of motets in **Mo** fascicle 7. While underlining his significance in theory and in practice, this chapter also seeks to contextualise Petrus, engaging with complex questions surrounding any definition of his corpus as well as the individuality of his rhythmic and notational techniques and his musical style. The book's fifth and final chapter examines motets built not on sacred plainchant tenors but on secular melodies, a late thirteenth-century species of motet to which **Mo** 7 and 8 are the principal witnesses. I suggest that this new type of tenor – in two instances actually labelled with the names of its creators, Tassin and Loyset – brings with it implications of authorship, which now pertains to all voices of a motet in a new way. **Mo**'s secular motet tenors preserve traces of instrumental and vernacular song traditions that were otherwise largely unwritten but, as I argue, much more significant and widespread than has previously been suspected. Although attributions and identifications are never explicit, **Mo**'s final fascicles are rich in largely unmined and unsuspected evidence about the identities and reception of thirteenth-century composers. These anonymous motet collections document musical lives, musical life, and indeed music – both polyphonic and monophonic – not otherwise committed to written record.

1 Adam de la Halle's Presence in the Final Fascicles of the Montpellier Codex

Little is known for certain about the life of Adam de la Halle, the cleric-trouvère from Arras, who is generally thought to have been born in the mid-1240s and to have died before 1290.[1] A total of five motets are attributed to him in the manuscript **Ha**, which opens with an author portrait of Adam, prefacing a comprehensive compilation of his works that is grouped by genre.[2] First come Adam's monophonic songs preceded by the rubric (on fol. 1v) 'Chi commencent les chanchons maistre Adan de la Hale'; the *jeux-partis* are announced as 'les partures Adan' (fol. 23v); 'li rondel Adan' – three-voice polyphonic rondeaux – begin on fol. 32v; and 'li motet Adan' (fol. 34v) mark the end of the collection's entirely musical contents, preceding dramatic *jeux* and poetic texts.[3] Such an authorial *opera omnia* is not at all unusual in the context of trouvère song manuscripts, although Adam's is somewhat remarkable in its scale and scope, as well as in its internal organisation by genre.[4] Its inclusion of polyphony is, however, wholly exceptional: **Ha** is the only extant trouvère author collection to contain groups of polyphonic works, and thus Adam is 'the only thirteenth-century trouvère to whom polyphony is explicitly attributed in a music manuscript'.[5]

---

1   For a recent view of Adam's dates – discussed in detail in Chapter 2 – see Symes 2019, 28–32.

2   See the discussion of the status of **Ha** as a true *opera omnia* in Saltzstein 2019a, 4–6. **Ha** omits a small number of works thought to be by Adam and includes several that are not by him (notably the *Jeu du pelerin*, discussed in Chapter 2, which – perhaps fictionally – announces Adam's death).

3   For a complete list of rubrics in Adam's compilation in **Ha**, see Huot 1987a, 67–68.

4   On authorial song collections, and in relation to Adam's *opera omnia*, see Haines 2019, esp. 112–20.

5   Saltzstein 2019a, 4. As Saltzstein notes (4 n. 16), several monophonic songs attributed to Gautier de Coinci have polyphonic concordances, but it seems unlikely that Gautier was the composer of these song melodies, still less of their polyphonic settings. The authorship of polyphonic settings remains an open question in the case of Guillaume d'Amiens: two

DOI: 10.4324/9781003259282-2

Adam cannot have been the only trouvère to operate in both monophonic and polyphonic spheres.[6] Yet even considering that other collections like **Ha** have been lost, the fact that **Ha** stands as a sole survival suggests that it was relatively unusual in its own time and that the creators of Adam's compilation flouted convention somewhat in including his rondeaux and motets.[7] Perhaps the compilers were particularly concerned to be comprehensive, or they especially valued Adam's polyphony, such that a place was found within **Ha** for motets usually reserved for motet books, and for polyphonic rondeaux that were not typically committed to permanent written record at all.[8] Whatever its motivation, **Ha** preserves the only known vernacular polyphonic author corpus of the thirteenth century that is explicitly framed as such, and it permits an unusually detailed engagement with Adam de la Halle's output and authorial persona.

Although Adam's identity is never openly declared in fascicle 7 of the motet collection in **Mo**, his presence as a compositional personality is undeniable. For a start, this fascicle contains three out of five of his known motets (see Table 1.1). Adam's pieces are not grouped together here, but all three of them betray the trace of his authorship, to greater or lesser extent. The triplum of *Entre Adam et Haniket/Chief bien seans/APTATUR* opens with his own name, and the motetus concludes 'que pris est Adans', observing

---

monophonic rondeaux attributed to him in **Vat** appear, without attribution, in a three-voice polyphonic context in **PaB**. On this, see Everist 2019, 333.

6 Notably, Saint-Cricq 2019 recently proposed that the trouvère Robert de Reims created polyphonic motets that were only later converted into monophonic songs. The author corpus for Philip the Chancellor in **LoB** also preserves both monophonic and polyphonic works, though exclusively in Latin, rather than the vernacular.

7 Owing to the anonymity of polyphonic sources, the reliability of polyphonic attributions to Adam in **Ha** is hard to verify. Two monophonic versions of polyphonic works by Adam in **Vat**, an author-ordered song-book with attributions, constitute the only known evidence. A copy of the middle voice of Adam's polyphonic rondeau *Dame, or sui* appears in **Vat** (fol. 55v) in the section of this manuscript devoted to Adam's songs and directly preceded by the rubric 'Adans' (Everist 2019, 333 n. 32, mistakenly states that the rondeau is unattributed here). However, the motetus voice of Adam's motet *J'os bien/Je n'os/IN SECULUM* (otherwise unique to **Ha**) is found later in **Vat** (fol. 93v, where staves for musical notation were never filled), at the end of the section devoted to the songs of Gillebert de Berneville. Although the motetus is not grouped with Adam's works earlier in the same book, it is notable that this piece is at the very end of Gillebert's collection, and *Je n'os* does not carry the usual authorial rubric that is typically reiterated at the beginning of each individual song.

8 Just three extant (late) thirteenth-century sources of polyphonic rondeaux are known: the sixteen rondeaux attributed to Adam in **Ha**; the fragmentary leaf **CaB**, which records a *jeu-parti* by Adam and the same first four of his polyphonic rondeaux in the same order as collected in **Ha** and seems to be a fragment of a similar author corpus; and the unnotated and unattributed collection of thirty-four polyphonic rondeau in **PaB**. On these sources, their dates, characteristics, and interrelationships, see Everist 1996.

Table 1.1 Motets attributed to Adam de la Halle

Motet (in **Ha** order)	Sources	No. of voices	Texted semibreves
Aucun se sont loe/ A Dieu commant/ SUPER TE	**Ha** **Mo** 7, no. 263	3	Triplum: 1 3-SB group, 33 2-SB groups Motetus: 1 2-SB group
De ma dame vient/ Dieus, comment porroie/ OMNES	**Ha** **Mo** 7, no. 279 **Bes**	3	Triplum: 21 2-SB groups Motetus: 3 2-SB groups
Entre Adam et Haniket/ Chief bien seans/ APTATUR	**Ha** **Mo** 7, no. 258 **Bes** **Ba** **Tu** **Vorau** Motetus text incipit cited with incorrect melody by Anonymous V, *De arte discantandi* (**StV**, fol. 275r, margin)	3	Triplum: 2 2-SB groups
J'os bien m'amie/ Je n'os a amie/ IN SECULUM	**Ha** **Vat** (motetus text only, staves for melody unfilled)	3	None
J'ai ades d'amours/ OMNES	**Ha**	2	None

that 'Adam was taken' by the beautiful beloved this text describes. Adam's name is absent from his two remaining motets in **Mo**, yet I argue later that both contain musico-textual signatures in the form of self-quotations from his polyphonic rondeaux. Compilers or users of **Mo** 7 could not have been oblivious to the authorship of these motets and their self-referential texts and quotations. And while Adam's motets are not contiguous in **Mo** 7, it is significant that this fascicle preserves a majority of them, since, as Table 1.1 shows, the dissemination of Adam's motets was otherwise modest.

With the exception of *Entre Adam/Chief bien seans/APTATUR*, preserved in six different manuscripts, none of Adam's motets is extant in more than three sources. **Ha** and **Mo** 7 are alone in recording three or more of Adam's five motets. **Bes**, a list of motetus incipits from a now lost late thirteenth-century collection of three-voice motets, is the only other source known to contain as many as two. **Mo** preserves what could be described as stylistically the most 'advanced' of Adam's compositions, the three of his pieces most in keeping with fascicle 7's repertoire of three-voice vernacular motets, in which fast-moving tripla with syllabically texted semibreves predominate.[9] By this token, the fact that Adam's corpus is incomplete here is unsurprising: constraints of manuscript layout alone would have made the inclusion of Adam's brief two-voice unicum *J'ai ades d'amours/OMNES* in **Mo** 7 an unorthodox choice. The three-voice *J'os bien m'amie/Je n'os a amie/IN SECULUM* would also have been relatively out of place in **Mo** 7 from a stylistic perspective, since its two highly florid upper voices move at the same rate and are consistently melismatic in their treatment of semibreves.[10] By contrast, pairs of texted semibreves consistently dominate the triplum of *Aucun se sont loe/A Dieu commant/SUPER TE*, with an additional lone group of three syllabic semibreves sung in the time of a breve.[11] Texted semibreve pairs are slightly less pervasive in the triplum of *De ma dame vient/Dieus, comment porroie/OMNES* and they are very sparingly used, appearing only twice, in *Entre Adam/Chief bien seans/APTATUR*. The order of Adam's five motets in **Ha** (maintained in Table 1.1) replicates exactly the succession of stylistic characteristics as profiled here, seemingly prioritising his most up-to-date compositions by beginning with *Aucun/A Dieu/SUPER TE* and closing with the two-voice *J'ai ades d'amours/OMNES*.

By far Adam's most copied polyphonic composition, *Entre Adam/Chief bien seans/APTATUR*, was the one in which his identity was most explicit. Adam, as author, seemingly held a certain status, since compilers of late thirteenth-century motet collections cared to include a piece that named him in both motetus and triplum texts and was (as discussed further in Chapter 3) stylistically on the old-fashioned side. On the one hand, compilers of motet manuscripts seem to have known Adam, but on the other, his motets were generally not that widely transmitted. This suggests that, even in the context of motet compilations, any name recognition was thanks largely to Adam's reputation as a composer of songs: either catchy tunes and polyphonic rondeaux whose circulation did not depend heavily on written sources, and/or the elevated corpus of thirty-six *grands chants* that were widely copied and of which none is a unicum.[12] Such wide dissemination of a substantial

---

9 Although many of the Latin double motets in **Mo** 7 (and **Mo** 8) are in a rhythmically modal style characteristic of the old corpus, the majority of the French-texted pieces are non-modal and/or make use of texted semibreves (principally pairs) in their tripla.

10 See the discussion and transcription of this motet in Everist 2019, 341–44.

11 See the discussion in Chapter 4 of the use of trios – as opposed to pairs – of texted semibreves.

12 See Ragnard 2019, 189–92.

output of *grands chants* stands in contrast to Adam's five motets, of which only **Ha** preserves a complete record. Nevertheless, a unique concentration of polyphony by and linked to Adam within the final fascicles of **Mo** – and especially in **Mo** 7 – underlines his authorial presence within the context of this anonymous motet collection.[13]

Ten motets are known to share textual and/or musical material with works securely attributed to Adam in **Ha** (see Table 1.2).[14] Two of these motets are by Adam himself, seven are anonymous, and one is by Petrus de Cruce. For two of these motets – Petrus's *Aucun ont trouve/Lonc tens/ ANNUN[TIANTES]* and the anonymous **Mo** 7 unicum *Entre Jehan et Philippet/Nus hom ne puet desiervir/CHOSE TASSIN*, the subject of Chapters 2 and 3 respectively – a connection to Adam is established here for the first time. The current chapter reconsiders the remaining eight compositions: the two motets by Adam himself that share refrains with his own rondeaux, and the six anonymous motets in **Mo** in which the presence of material elsewhere ascribed to Adam has long been acknowledged. It engages analytically with questions of chronology in order to challenge the accepted view that Adam was more likely to have been familiar with the repertoire of motets in **Mo** fascicle 7 than that composers of **Mo** 7 motets knew Adam's rondeaux.[15] This serves to rethink Adam's status within **Mo**, demonstrating him not merely to be a borrower from this motet repertoire, but rather an author known and invoked – in various ways and to various ends – by motet creators.

---

13 As discussed later, eight anonymous and unattributed motets contain musical and/or textual material by Adam (see Table 1.2). Seven are found in **Mo** 7 with one in **Mo** 8: three of these pieces are unica in **Mo**, three survive in only one other manuscript, and the remaining two pieces are extant in just two further sources.

14 I do not count as a quotation the appearance of Adam's polyphonic rondeau refrain text vdB 784 within the **Mo** motet *Que ferai/Ne puet faillir/DESCENDENTIBUS* (copied twice in **Mo** fascicle 5, as nos. 77 and 144). This refrain text, '*Hareu li maus d'amer m'ochist*', is both widespread and generic. That it appears with a different melody in its rondeau and motet contexts distinguishes it from all other of the quotations of Adam's rondeau in **Mo** motets discussed here.

15 Everist 1996, 88–89 reprinted in Everist 2019, 329 (subsequent references cite only the re-worked 2019 version). Saltzstein deliberately avoids chronological judgement about quotations of or by Adam; see Saltzstein 2013, 127–29, 135–39, and 141–47. Yet she is generally sympathetic to Everist's proposed precedence for the repertoire of **Mo** 7 (see 129). The recent examination of refrains in Adam's output in Ibos-Augé 2019 does not engage directly with chronological questions.

Table 1.2 Motets quoting material attributed to Adam

Motet (each section follows **Mo** order)	Sources	Type of quoted material	Location of quotation	Quoted material and sources	vdB no.
Adam's motet quotations of his own rondeau refrains					
Aucun se sont loe/ A Dieu commant/ SUPER TE (Adam de la Halle)	**Ha** Mo 7, no. 263	Polyphonic rondeau refrain	All 3 voices, enté presentation at opening and close	A Dieu commant (unique **Ha**)	12
De ma dame vient/ Dieus, comment porroie/ OMNES (Adam de la Halle)	**Ha** Mo 7, no. 279 **Bes**	Middle voice of polyphonic rondeau refrain	Motetus, enté presentation at opening and internal (down a tone)	Dieus, comment porroie (unique **Ha**)	496
Anonymous motets quoting Adams's rondeaux					
Mout me fu grief/ Robin m'aime/ PORTARE	**Mo** 7, no. 265 **Ba** **Bes**	Monophonic rondeau from Jeu de Robin et Marion	Motetus, throughout (up a 5th)	Jeu de Robin et Marion (**Ha**, **Méjanes**, text only in **Fr. 1569**)	1633
En mai/ L'autre jour/ HE RESVEILLE TOI ROBIN	**Mo** 7, no. 269 **Reg** **Bes**	Monophonic refrain from Jeu de Robin et Marion	Tenor, throughout	Jeu de Robin et Marion (**Ha**, **Méjanes**, text only in **Fr. 1569**)	870
Dame bele/ Fi, mari/ NUS N'IERT JA JOLIS	**Mo** 7, no. 271 **Reg**	Polyphonic rondeau refrain	All 3 voices, opening	Fi, mari (unique **Ha**)	746

Bien met amours/ Dame, alegies ma grevance/ A PARIS [*sic*, for *APERIS*]	**Mo** 7, no. 291 **Bes**	Middle voice of polyphonic rondeau refrain	Triplum, internal quotation (near end)	*He, Dieus, quant verrai* (unique **Ha**)	823
Theotheca, virgo geratica/ Las, pour qoi/ QUI PRANDROIT	**Mo** 7, no. 302 (supplement 2)	Middle voice of polyphonic rondeau refrain	Triplum, end	*He, Dieus, quant verrai* (unique **Ha**)	823
Motets quoting Adam's motets					
Aucun ont trouvé/ Lonc tens/ ANNUN[TIANTES] (Petrus de Cruce)	**Mo** 7, no. 254 **Tu**	Text and music of triplum incipit *Aucun se*	Triplum, opening	*Aucun se sont loe/ A Dieu comment/ SUPER TE* (**Ha**, **Mo** 7)	N/a
Entre Jehan et Philippet/ Nus hom ne puet desiervir/ CHOSE TASSIN	**Mo** 7, no. 294 (supplement 1)	Text only of triplum *Entre Adam et Haniket*	Triplum text, throughout	*Entre Adam et Haniket/ Chief bien seans/ APTATUR* (**Ha**, **Mo** 7, **Bes**, **Ba**, **Tu**, **Vorau**)	N/a
Se je sui/ Jolietement/ OMNES	**Mo** 8, no. 316	Text and music of motetus incipit *Chief bien seans*	Triplum, end (up a 5th)	*Entre Adam et Haniket/ Chief bien seans/ APTATUR* (**Ha**, **Mo** 7, **Bes**, **Ba**, **Tu**, **Vorau**)	N/a

Self-quotation in Adam's **Mo** **Motets**

That a tendency to quote Adam in motets was a precedent set by Adam himself is suggested by the circumstances of his own *Aucun/A Dieu/SUPER TE*. Beyond the group of Adam's five motets in **Ha**, this motet is found only in **Mo** 7, without authorial attribution.[16] The motetus voice presents a refrain text and melody (vdB 12) employed in the middle voice of the three-part polyphonic rondeau *A Dieu commant*, uniquely preseved in **Ha** (on fol. 33r) among Adam's sixteen rondeaux.[17] In Adam's motetus, the A and B material of his rondeau refrain are presented in the split manner of the *motet enté*: the A material is placed at the beginning of the motetus and the B material at its conclusion, with new music 'grafted' between them. Example 1.1 gives the refrain of Adam's rondeau and Example 1.2 shows the corresponding portion of *Aucun/A Dieu/SUPER TE* – the beginning and end of the motet – as recorded in **Ha**.[18] The middle voices of the two compositions, presenting the same refrain, are musically and textually identical, and – as previously noted by Friedrich Ludwig, Jennifer Saltzstein, and Anne Ibos-Augé – the two lowest voices are also undoubtedly related.[19] There are only four differences of pitch between the lowest voice of the rondeau and the motet tenor and all are on unstressed breves (marked by boxes in Examples 1.1 and 1.2). There are two additional instances, also both on unstressed breves, in which a pitch sounding in the lowest voice of the rondeau corresponds to a rest in the motet tenor (marked by wavy boxes in Examples 1.1 and 1.2). Although the respective triplum voices are largely independent, their similar musical

16 Saltzstein 2013, 138, noted that, while one of the texts in this motet begins with the word 'Aucun' (some) in the piece as recorded in **Mo**, this opening word in **Ha** is instead rendered 'Adam', an explicit nod to the motet's composer. Everist 2019, 347, develops a further authorial interpretation of the **Ha** version on this basis. I have rejected this hypothesis on palaeographical grounds; see Bradley 2020, 493.

17 VdB 12 appears exclusively in these two works by Adam and its text is autobiographical: see Saltzstein 2013, 135–48. Ibos-Augé 2019, 267–68, has recently drawn attention to musical and textual similarities between vdB 12 and vdB 13, suggesting that Adam's refrain was a personal adaptation of the more widely transmitted vdB 13.

18 In this motet in **Ha**, the voice *A Dieu commant* is copied first, in the normal position of a motet triplum, followed by *Aucun se sont loe*, in the normal position of the motetus. Registrally, however, *Aucun se sont loe* is the higher voice and it appears in the triplum position in the only other extant copy of the same motet in **Mo**. Everist 2019, 346, convincingly proposes that this exchange of the order of the voice parts in **Ha**, with the consequence that Adam's motet section opens with *A Dieu commant*, draws attention to the link with this rondeau. Example 1.2 retains the order of motet voices in **Mo**, swapping the order of the voices as they appear in **Ha**.

19 Ludwig 1978, 431; Saltzstein 2013, 136; Ibos-Augé 2019, 266–67.

Example 1.1 Adam de la Halle, refrain of polyphonic rondeau *A Dieu commant*, **Ha**, fol. 33r

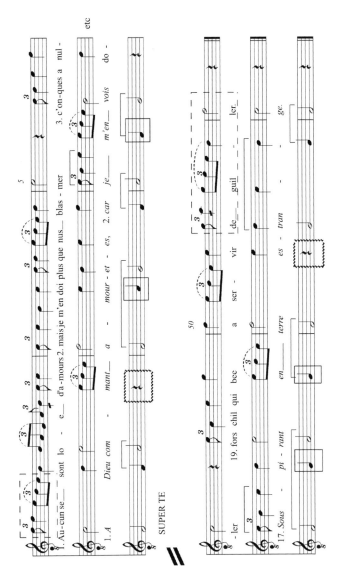

Example 1.2 Adam de la Halle, motet *Aucun se sont loe/A Dieu commant/SUPER TE*, **Ha**, fols. 34v–35r, perfections 1–6 and 48–52

incipits and explicits (marked by dashed boxes in Examples 1.1 and 1.2) suggest that this aspect of the polyphonic complex was related too.

That one of these compositions is modelled (polyphonically) on the other is therefore clear. But the quotational direction – from rondeau to motet or from motet to rondeau – has not been established with certainty. Conventionally, the priority of a monophonic rondeau as the origin of a refrain has generally been preferred, in view of both the inherent structural role of the refrain in this genre and long-established historiographical narratives that placed the origins of refrains in rondeaux and dance songs, rather than in motets.[20] Sylvia Huot's poetic reading of this rondeau and motet by Adam is in sympathy with the conventional chronology, considering the motet text as an amplification of its related rondeau, where the *je* of the rondeau's single departing lover is expanded in Adam's motet to encompass the community of Arras.[21]

More recent scholarship has tended to favour the reverse relationship in cases of polyphonic concordances between motets and rondeaux: that Adam's polyphonic rondeaux derived from his motets. In an attempt to challenge older conceptualisations of Adam's polyphonic rondeaux as popular dance songs, Ardis Butterfield suggested that Adam's rondeaux should be viewed 'as a response to experiments with refrains in polyphony in the genre of the motet'.[22] Similarly, though perhaps in deference to the motet's more established status as a polyphonic genre, Robert Falck tentatively posited a polyphonic 'interdependence' between rondeau and motet as an indication that Adam's rondeau was based on the motet.[23] Although Mark Everist deliberately left open chronological questions about the status of *A Dieu commant* and *Aucun/A Dieu/SUPER TE*, he nonetheless, as emphasised earlier, preferred in general to ascribe priority to the motets in fascicle 7 of **Mo** – proposing that Adam was familiar with this repertoire – rather than to Adam's rondeaux.

On musical and analytical grounds, however, the priority of the rondeau is most convincing in the case of *A Dieu commant*.[24] In the rondeau, the refrain's B material is musically identical to the beginning of the A material in all three

---

20 For a summary (and critique) of these refrain origin narratives, see Saltzstein 2013, 10–16.

21 Huot 1987b, 156–57.

22 Butterfield 2002, 283.

23 Robert Falck, 'Adam de la Halle', *Grove Music Online* (accessed 27 Mar. 2020), https://doi.org/10.1093/gmo/9781561592630.article.00163. Falck makes this remark in specific reference to Adam's rondeau *Fi, mari* and the motet *Dame bele/Fi, mari/NUS N'IERT JA JOLIS*, discussed in detail later.

24 Dissonance is not a useful chronological indicator here, since the first lowest voice variant results in a more consonant reading in the motet version, and the second produces a more dissonant reading in the motet version (that is avoided in the copy of the motet in **Mo** by a less exact quotation of the motetus refrain). On harmonic and textural differences between polyphonic rondeaux and motets in general, see Bradley 2019, 473–75.

voices, diverging only at the cadence. In the motet, however, the melodic relationship between the A and B sections of the motetus refrain is obscured by the fact that they appear in different harmonic and rhythmic tenor contexts. This change in the refrain's polyphonic context is demanded by the melodic sequence and rhythmic pattern of the tenor plainchant quotation. Had the motet been Adam's initial creation, extra pitches would have had to have been added to the lowest voice of the rondeau in order to support its syllabic text, but there would have been no need to alter any pitches, which could simply have reproduced the melody of the motet tenor exactly.[25] By contrast, the alteration of tenor pitches would have been required in a conversion from rondeau to motet, where Adam's choice of pitches was – again – constrained by a plainchant quotation. In general, Adam's works in **Ha** seem to have been carefully cross-referenced, and refrains found in multiple compositions usually appear in exactly the same form (as in the case of *A Dieu commant*).[26] It is especially likely, then, that had the direction of quotation been from motet to rondeau, the lowest voice of Adam's rondeau would have reproduced as exactly as possible the plainchant tenor of a parent motet.

Until recently, the status of the motet tenor SUPER TE as a genuine plainchant melody remained in doubt, since a liturgical source for this unique polyphonic tenor had not been identified.[27] My discovery of an exact match for Adam's SUPER TE tenor, with the melody accompanying the words 'super te orta est' within the responsory for Matins on the Feast of Epiphany, *Illuminare illuminare Iherusalem. Et ambulabunt*, has proved its quotational status.[28] Adam's choice of the long-unidentified motet tenor SUPER TE – drawn from a chant that appears nowhere in the polyphonic repertoire of the earlier Parisian *Magnus liber* or in any other extant motet – itself requires some justification. The tenor was unfamiliar to the scribe of the **Mo** 7, who labelled the lowest voice of Adam's motet ET SUPER, the name of a different chant melody used in four other motets in **Mo**. This mislabelling may well have

---

25 With specific reference to this example, Butterfield 2002, 282, observed that the 'tenor of a rondeau is often a lightly expanded version of the corresponding motet'. But this does not account for the changes of pitch in the portions of the motet tenor that do not require expansion.

26 On the consistency of refrain identities across **Ha**, see Everist 2019, 330–31. See also Butterfield 1991, 13–15. On the stability of polyphonic rondeaux as quotable entitles, see Bradley 2019, 474–75.

27 On the lack of an identified plainchant source for the SUPER TE tenor, see Saltzstein 2013, 136. It is possible that the connection of the SUPER TE ORTA EST plainchant melisma with Adam's tenor was made – though never explicitly stated – by Tischler. In his edition of *Aucun se sont loe/A Dieu commant/SUPER TE*, Tischler supplies the editorial tenor text SUPER TE ORTA EST, though **Mo** has (erroneously) ET SUPER, and the only other copy of the motet, in **Ha**, gives merely SUPER TE. See Tischler 1978, vol. 3, 84–85 (no. 263).

28 See Bradley 2019, 466–67.

been the scribe's own 'correction'. Like SUPER TE, the ET SUPER tenor melody begins on F, the chant's final or home pitch. Given the similarity of the two tenor labels, the scribe plausibly took the formulation SUPER TE to be an error, having encountered it nowhere else in the manuscript.

It is all the less likely that Adam would scrupulously preserve, as a rondeau tenor, the contour of an unusual plainchant quotation, evidently unrecognisable to the thirteenth-century scribe at work in **Mo** 7. It is more plausible that he instead sought out a plainchant melisma that offered as similar as possible a harmonic foundation to the lowest voice of his existing rondeau, and – in order to find one – was forced to choose from outside the range of established polyphonic tenors. A well-educated and musical cleric such as Adam would have had considerable familiarity with liturgical plainchant melodies and thus be able to recall a melisma that, like his rondeau tenor, predominantly circled around the pitches F, G, and a.[29] The choice of the SUPER TE melisma was an ingenuious solution, since it could be quoted without melodic alteration and arranged in a consistent rhythmic pattern.

Adam's inauguration of the SUPER TE tenor is in keeping with a subtle awareness of conventions for plainchant quotation in polyphony that is evident in his motet *De ma dame/Dieus, comment/OMNES*. This motet – in **Bes**, as well as in **Ha** and **Mo** 7 – is unique in the thirteenth-century repertoire because it exploits different established versions of the OMNES tenor within a single piece. The motet uses two alternative incarnations of this tenor – with three and two internal iterations of the pitch F respectively – to facilitate the motet's myriad upper-voice quotations.[30] *De ma dame/Dieus, comment/ OMNES* quotes four different refrains in total and, as Ibos-Augé recently observed, unusually complements and highlights these refrain quotations by the rhythmically (as well as melodically) varied structure of its underlying chant tenor.[31] Adam's motet opens with a simultaneous triple quotation of the chant melody OMNES in the tenor, the widely circulating refrain '*De ma dame*' (vdB 477) in the triplum, and in the motetus the middle voice of the first half of his own rondeau refrain '*Dieus, comment porroie*' (vdB 496).

The way in which Adam's rondeau refrain is split in his motet confirms that this is the quotation rather than the source: the opening refrain is completed mid-motetus, and here introduced by a reiteration of the words 'comment porroie' but set to different music.[32] It is unlikely that Adam would

---

29 On Adam's clerical status and his academic title 'maistre', see Corbellari 2019.
30 On established versions of the OMNES tenor, see Bradley 2019, 452–55.
31 See Ibos-Augé 2019, 268–71.
32 Outside Adam's motet and rondeau, vdB 496 also appears, with music, in two copies of the romance *Renart le nouvel*, **Renart C** and **Renart F** (but is notably absent from the copy of *Renart* in **Ha**). The melodies in the two copies are different. Furthermore, two different

have joined together two parts of a motetus voice so disparate in presentation, and whose status as a unit was rather disguised, in order to create his rondeau refrain. Moreover, it seems that the refrain was also transposed down a tone to start on f in the motet version (rather than g, as in the polyphonic rondeau) to suit the OMNES tenor. Adam's self-quotation does not preserve its polyphonic context in this motet, and arguably this was made impossible, at least at the motet's outset, because of its combination with another refrain quotation in the triplum. But polyphonic quotation does occur for the motetus's concluding refrain. As Saltzstein has shown, Adam's motetus closes with the widely disseminated refrain vdB 1473, presenting it in exactly the same tenor context as in the motet *Tant me fait/Tout li cuers/ OMNES*, recorded in **Mo**'s old corpus (fascicle 5, no. 115) and in **Ba**.[33]

As in *Aucun/A Dieu/SUPER TE*, Adam took the harmonic context of a quoted refrain into consideration in *De ma dame/Dieus, comment/OMNES*, thereby increasing – as Saltzstein has suggested – the chances that this quotation was heard and perceived.[34] *De ma dame/Dieus, comment/OMNES* confirms Adam's facility and compositional interest in quotation, of refrains and tenor plainchants alike, and in the musical combination of such quotations, as well as in quoting polyphonically and in quoting his own refrains. Adam's self-quotations in *Aucun/A Dieu/SUPER TE* and *De ma dame/Dieus, comment/OMNES* are a less explicit means of self-identification than the straightforward inclusion of his own name in *Entre Adam/Chief bien seans/APTATUR*. Nevertheless, it is possible – especially in the case of the polyphonic self-quotation in *Aucun/A Dieu/SUPER TE* – that they were recognisable as musico-poetic signatures, even in the context of an outwardly anonymous motet collection such as **Mo**.

Adam's Rondeaux in Anonymous Mo Motets

Quoting Adam's Jeu de Robin et Marion*:* Robin m'aime *and* He resveille toi

Adam's presence is most concentrated within the main body of **Mo** fascicle 7, where all three of his own motets appear, alongside four further

---

versions of the refrain are presented at different points in the romance in **Renart C**. The first appearance of vdB 496 in **Renart C** resembles the refrain in Adam's polyphonic rondeau, and it is therefore possible that Adam's rondeau was modelled on an existing refrain. Nevertheless, the closest connection between extant versions of vdB 496 is unquestionably that between Adam's rondeau and motet: clearly, one of these compositions quoted the refrain directly from the other.

33 Saltzstein 2013, 127–30. See also the discussion in Bradley 2019, 459 n. 68.
34 See Saltzstein 2013, 137.

anonymous pieces that, as demonstrated later, quote refrains associated with Adam.[35] The first two of these anonymous motets refer, respectively, to a monophonic rondeau and a refrain found among the musical interpolations in Adam's dramatic *Jeu de Robin et Marion*. In the first instance at least, quotation is unmistakable. *Mout me fu grief/Robin m'aime/PORTARE* adopts, as its motetus voice, the complete opening rondeau of Adam's *Jeu* (compare Examples 1.3 and 1.4).[36] As Dolores Pesce has shown, the quotation of *Robin m'aime* requires considerable musical accommodation in the motet context, where the melody of the PORTARE chant quotation in the tenor is radically adapted to the motetus's rondeau form.[37]

The motet transposes Adam's rondeau melody up a fifth and adds melodic decorations (marked by boxes in Example 1.4), but the material is otherwise musically very stable between the two versions. By contrast, the middle lines of the rondeau text vary (compare lines 3–5 in Examples 1.3 and 1.4).[38] While both *Jeu* and motet describe the gifts given to Marion by Robin, they do so using differing vocabulary and rhyme endings. In the motet context, it is hard to posit a poetic motivation for this alternative text, either semantically or structurally, since the rondeau's internal rhymes in neither the *Jeu* nor the motetus are shared with the motet triplum.[39] Such internal textual variation is striking in the face of the musical and textual stability of the refrain material, but it is more understandable when the rondeau is considered from the perspective of its performance and indeed of a possibly oral or memory-based transmission.[40]

It is hardly surprising that the framing refrain – whose text Adam himself may have quoted – should be the most stable element of the rondeau.[41] The

---

35 Works by and/or linked to Adam are not contiguous in **Mo** 7, although some are relatively proximate with a cluster of four – no. 263 (by Adam) and the anonymous nos. 265, 269, and 271 – around the middle of the fascicle proper.

36 The overall rondeau from is ABaabAB, omitting the conventional internal return of the first half of the rondeau melody accompanied by its refrain text. This is the only complete rondeau in Adam's *Jeu*, which contains just two other repetitive songs of extended length. These two songs are much further from any conventional rondeau form: Grau 2019, 298, recently characterised them as '*pastourelles-ballettes*'.

37 See Pesce 1997, 29. For a confirmation of this chronology, see also Thomson 2017, 137–40.

38 On textual variants, see Ludwig 1978, 432; Thomson 2016, 35–36.

39 The only material difference between the two texts is that, whereas the rondeau in the *Jeu* devotes more space to describing Robin's gifts, the motetus rondeau makes explicit their consequence, concluding 'why then would I not love him'.

40 On the slightly different relationship between refrains and *additamenta* in *rondets de carole*, questions of relative stability, and literate and oral transmission, see Butterfield 2002, 45–49.

41 Adam seems to have adopted this refrain text (vdB 1663), and others in the *Jeu de Robin et Marion*, from the pastourelle *Au tens nouvel* (RS 573) by the trouvère Perrin d'Angicourt, also from Arras. See Saltzstein 2008, 183; Ibos-Augé 2019, 274–75.

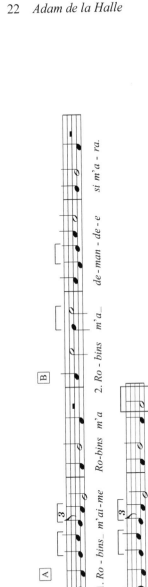
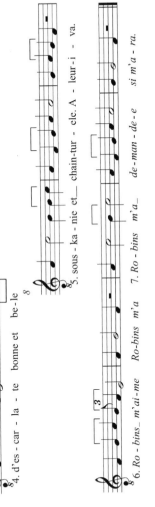

Example 1.3 Adam de la Halle, rondeau *Robin m'aime*, **Ha**, fol. 39r

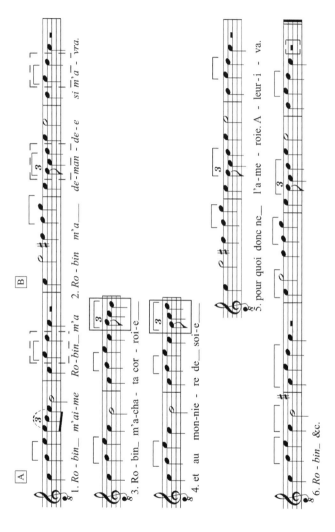

Example 1.4 Motetus of *Mout me fu grief/Robin m'aime/PORTARE*, **Mo** 7, fols. 292r–293r

two parts of its melody (labelled A and B) are subject to continual repetition, and its text is also repeated and is itself memorably repetitive: '*Robin m'aime, Robin m'a/Robin m'a demandee, si m'avra*'. By contrast, the rondeau's internal poetic material, sung only once and here fairly generic in its semantic content, is the more likely to be forgotten. Notably, the motet text matches the opening of the first of the *Jeu*'s internal lines – line 3, 'Robins m'acata' (Robin bought me) – which itself replicates the sounds of the refrain opening and is also crucial in setting up the narrative, initiating the list of gifts that varies between *Jeu* and motet versions. Following this list, the nonsense exclamation 'Aleuriva' (at the end of line 5), which reintroduces the refrain's end-rhyme and leads back to the rondeau refrain, is again identical in both texts. This suggests that the motet quotes a rondeau known from performance or committed to memory rather than accessed in a written form: the music and text of the framing refrain sticks in the mind, and the immediate links to get out of and back into this refrain – and which are most closely connected to it poetically – are retained. The lines in the middle of the text, which are poetically more generic and less tightly connected by rhyme to the refrain material, are less memorable and/or more interchangeable.

The two extant sources of *Mout me fu grief/Robin m'aime/PORTARE* in **Mo** and **Ba** agree closely on their musical and textual version of the *Robin m'aime* motetus. Likewise, the copy of Adam's *Jeu* in **Fr. 1569**, where space was left for musical notation that was never entered, matches precisely the text of the rondeau interpolation in **Ha**. Yet a third extant version of this rondeau in the copy of the *Jeu* that opens the lavishly illuminated fourteenth-century manuscript **Méjanes** tellingly shares features of both *Jeu* and motetus versions.[42] Melodically, the **Méjanes** refrain is closer in its extra decorative details to the transposed *Robin m'aime* motetus than to the (untransposed) version in **Ha** (shared decorations are marked by dashed boxes in Examples 1.4 and 1.5).[43] Textually, however, **Méjanes** broadly follows **Ha** but with some additional and revealing departures. While Marion's dress is of fine light fabric in **Ha** ('d'escarlate', at the opening of line 4), it is coarser and darker in **Méjanes** ('de burel'). But more importantly, **Méjanes** cuts short the description of Robin's gifts, simply omitting altogether the beginning of the refrain's B material in line 5 and jumping straight to the line's concluding 'Aleuriva'.

42 On **Méjanes**, its date and decoration, see Cruse, Parussa, and Ragnard 2004.
43 Ibos-Augé 2018b, 258, also offers a paradigmatic transcription of this version of the rondeau. She conceives the form as AB A'A'A'A AB (rather than AB AAB' AB, as in Example 1.5). This understanding of the form is, however, based on a misreading of the pitch accompanying the '-leur' of 'Aleuriva' as F, rather than G, which allows Ibos-Augé to conflate this shortened B material (B') with the ending of a complete statement of A (which, in fact, has a subtly different cadence).

Example 1.5 Adam de la Halle, rondeau *Robin m'aime*, **Méjanes**, fol. 1r

In order to make this cut, **Méjanes** exploits a melodic technique that, again, seems closer to the *Robin m'aime* motetus than to the rondeau in **Ha**. In all extant versions, lines 3 and 4 of the rondeau gain an extra syllable of text by replacing the concluding rest of the refrain's A material with an additional pitch. In **Ha** this simply is a repetition of the preceding F (marked by boxes in Example 1.3). In **Méjanes** the extra pitch is, instead, E (marked by boxes in Example 1.5), with the result that the internal A phrases end with a semitonal descent to a leading note that links more strongly to the beginning of the next phrase, where it achieves resolution.[44] The endings of lines 3 and 4 in the *Robin m'aime* motetus exploit essentially the same technique (marked by boxes in Example 1.4), each concluding with a different decorated figure that ends on a neighbour-note pitch which resolves at the beginning of the next phrase. It is this cadential link that facilitates and integrates the cut – the unconventional elision of the A material with the end of the B material between lines 4 and 5 – in the **Méjanes** version. The first note of the 'Aleuriva' B material in line 5 is altered, from a to E, to stand in for the final pitch of the A material in line 4, replicating the ending of line 3.

All of these features of **Méjanes** are suggestive of a fundamentally performative culture surrounding the transmission of Adam's rondeau. The framing refrain and the texts that lead out of and back into it are faithfully retained, while internal material is varied and here even excised. The endings of the rondeau's internal A repetitions are subtly adapted musically in a way that seems performatively very intuitive, and which creates more tonally directed links between phrases. This version of the *Robin m'aime* rondeau more concretely encapsulates the kinds of performative traces already visible in its motetus incarnation. It is an important reminder that, although **Ha** stands as vital written testament to Adam's output and achieves a notably high degree of internal consistency when any musical and poetic material is repeated across the manuscript, Adam's catchy melodies were probably more often, sung, heard, and remembered.

A wider oral circulation of Adam's rondeaux than extant written records attest would account not only for their relatively extensive quotation but also for the circumstances of the second motet in **Mo** that apparently borrows material from Adam's *Jeu*. This is *En mai/L'autre jour/HE RESVEILLE TOI ROBIN*, which adopts as its tenor the refrain '*He resveille toi Robin*' (vdB 870), a musical interpolation that appears towards the end of Adam's *Jeu de Robin et Marion*.[45] In the motet context, the very location

---

44 This replicates the same F – E – F progression that facilitates internal melodic and poetic repetition within the A material itself (between '*Robin m'aime*' and '*Robin m'a*').

45 On the transmission of vdB 870, see also Ibos-Augé 2019, 277–78. On this motet and its broader textual interactions with the refrain vdB 870, in Adam's *Jeu* and beyond, see Butterfield 2011, 218–21. See also the discussion of the various interpretative contexts of, and invoked by, vdB 870 in Saltzstein 2008, 176–83.

He res-veil-le toi Ro-bin   car on en mai - ne Ma-rot.   Car on en mai - ne___Mar-ot.

Example 1.6 Adam de la Halle, refrain interpolation *He resveille toi* in *Jeu de Robin et Marion*, **Ha**, fol. 43r

of this refrain in the tenor part – the motet voice invariably reserved for pre-existing musical and textual material – is already an indication that it was understood and intended to be perceived as a quotation. As Saltzstein has demonstrated, however, this same refrain text appears twice beyond the context of Adam's works and – as in the case of *Robin m'aime* – was probably borrowed, rather than created by Adam himself.[46] The question arises, therefore, as to whether or not the pre-existing refrain on which the **Mo** 7 motet was built carried with it the association of Adam's identity.

Since Adam's *Jeu* and the **Mo** 7 motet tenor are the only notated sources of the *He resveille toi* refrain, any dependence on a pre-existing melody as well as a pre-existing text cannot be established.[47] Yet these two musically near-identical versions of the refrain are set apart from all other poetic survivals by their unique form of the refrain text, in which the second half of the refrain's AB-form couplet is repeated to give the tripartite text form ABB. The refrain melody complements this tripartite design with an ABB′ form, in which the first A section ends with a 'closed' cadence on G, the first B section ends on an 'open' a, and the final B′ section repeats the previous B phrase but leading now to a 'closed' cadence on G (see Example 1.6).[48] Ibos-Augé has emphasised that tripartite refrains like this one, in which text and music complement one another structurally, are vanishingly rare in the refrain corpus as a whole. In the context of Adam's *Jeu de Robin et Marion*, however, such repetitive refrains are typical, and the *Jeu* contains four tripartite refrains of precisely this type, half of all known examples.[49]

46 See Saltzstein 2019b, 358–59; Saltzstein 2008, 182–83. Saltzstein emphasises that vdB 870 is probably (and like *Robin m'aime*) an Arras refrain, this time by Huitace de Fontaines, and that by quoting it Adam underlines his local lineage.
47 Only the middle of the triplum voice survives in the fragmentary concordance for this motet in **Reg**.
48 The version of the same refrain in **Méjanes** (fol. 6r) is musically and textually identical to that in **Ha**, apart from the fact that it is transposed up a fifth (to begin on d).
49 Ibos-Augé 2019, 278 n. 55. Of these four tripartite refrains, one (vdB 252) is part of a larger repetitive song in this context, but the other three (vdB 870, 1161, and 1835) are stand-alone refrain interpolations. See also Grau 2019, 302 on the expansive and repetitive nature of refrains in *Jeu de Robin et Marion*, which stand in contrast to those in *Renart le nouvel*.

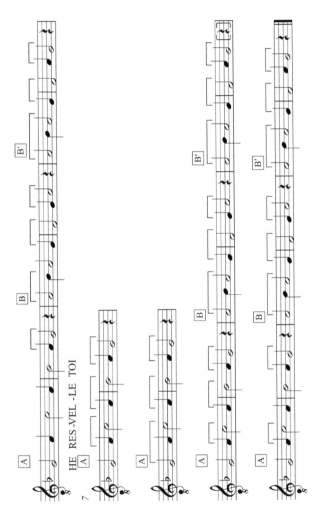

Example 1.7 Tenor of *En mai/L'autre jour/HE RESVEILLE TOI* motet, **Mo** 7, fols. 297r–298v

Moreover, Adam's polyphonic rondeau *Or est baiars* (preserved uniquely in **Ha**, fol. 33v) is also built on a refrain with a poetic and musical ABB form.

This suggests not only that the tripartite version of the *He resveille toi* refrain was Adam's invention, but that it was expressly (re)fashioned by him, in the same vein as other refrain interpolations in his *Jeu*. Consequently, the tenor of *En mai/L'autre jour /HE RESVEILLE TOI* is not merely a quotation of a pre-existing refrain, but more likely a quotation specifically of Adam's version of it.[50] However, this motet tenor does not – as is typical for motets based on refrains – straightforwardly state or reiterate Adam's refrain.[51] Rather the HE RESVEILLE TOI tenor takes the shape of a complete and entirely conventional rondeau: if the paired B material (B and B') is considered as a single unit, the musical form of the motet tenor is AB AA AB AB (see Example 1.7).[52] Unfortunately, **Mo** is the only fully extant source of this motet and – as is typical in this manuscript – gives no more than the initial tenor text incipit, which cannot inform as to the existence or content of a complete rondeau poem. Although no such evidence survives, it is probable for several reasons that *He resveille toi* circulated independently of this motet tenor not only as a refrain but as a complete monophonic rondeau.[53] As Everist and Matthew P. Thompson have emphasised, the rondeau form of the tenor assumes considerable importance in the motet composition, where it is fundamental in shaping the upper voices, which mirror and complement their underlying tenor structure.[54] In the context of song tenors (a corpus detailed in Table 5.1) HE RESVEILLE TOI is anomalous: there is no other example of a motet tenor based on a refrain that is in a tripartite form and concludes with an extended B section featuring an internal text repetition. It is therefore unlikely that the creator of *En mai/L'autre jour/HE RESVEILLE TOI* would have selected such an atypical refrain in order – and again unusually – to generate a new rondeau-form motet tenor. By contrast, such refrains are characteristic within Adam's oeuvre and a rondeau of this precise and otherwise abnormal formal type survives within his (polyphonic) corpus. It is probable, therefore, that the rondeau *He resveille toi*, now known only as a

---

50 The discussion of this motet in Saltzstein 2008, 180, assumes an alternative chronology: that the motet tenor is a quotation of a pre-existing refrain subsequently quoted by Adam. Saltzstein does not, however, note the unusual tripartite form of vdB 870 nor that this characteristic is common to other refrains in Adam's *Jeu*.

51 A single refrain is straightforwardly repeated in the tenor of *Tres joliement/Imperatrix/CIS A CUI JE SUI AMIE* (**Mo** 7, no. 272), for example.

52 On the (rondeau) form of the HE RESVEILLE TOI tenor, see also Thomson 2016, 42 and 44 n. 41. The transcription of the motet tenor in Saltzstein 2008, 181 omits an internal repetition of the A material, with the result that the rondeau form is given incorrectly (180) as ABAABAB.

53 See Thomson 2016, 43, for a more circumspect position on the existence of a monophonic rondeau based on vdB 870.

54 See Everist 2007, 386; Thomson 2016, 44–49.

Example 1.8 Refrain of polyphonic virelai *Prenes l'abre*, **Ivrea**, fol. 28r

motet tenor, did indeed have a genuine independent existence as a song, and one at least associated with, if not known to be by, Adam.[55]

Remarkably, *He resveille toi* makes a further appearance in its tripartite refrain form – but not its rondeau incarnation – in the later fourteenth-century collection of motets and songs in **Ivrea**.[56] Wyndham Thomas first identified Adam's version of this refrain, here simply labelled 'tenor', with the lowest voice of the refrain (or A) section of the unique and anonymous two-voice virelai *Prenes l'abre* (see Example 1.8).[57] In this tenor, the A section of Adam's refrain is altered: it is extended by the internal insertion of extra pitches (marked by a box in Example 1.8) and its concluding pitches are differently rhythmicised. The tenor's B and B' sections are, however, an exact match for Adam's refrain, save the introduction of a single decorative pitch at the outset of B (boxed in Example 1.8). The **Ivrea** tenor presents the refrain rhythmically at the level of breves and semibreves (such that a perfect breve – rather than a perfect long – now corresponds to a dotted minim in Example 1.8), rather than the original longs and breves of all of the other thirteenth-century sources. This alters the abstract rhythmic values and written appearance of the refrain, but the essence of the original rhythmic durations are thereby maintained. As explicitly outlined by Jacobus, the fourteenth-century 'moderns' – owing to their penchant for many short notes – favoured a slower overall tempo, such that the perfect longs and breves of the 'ancients' were now effectively equivalent in length to the perfect breves and semibreves of the moderns.[58]

Evidence, in practice, of notational 'translation' between old and new tempos is relatively rare. One of few known examples concerns the motet *Exaudi melodiam/Alme Deus/[TENOR]*, which – as Elizabeth Eva Leach has demonstrated – survives in 'Ars antiqua' notation in **Dijon 447** and in 'Ars nova' notation in **StM**.[59] In this case, the translation went awry, because although longs and breves were exchanged for imperfect breves and semibreves in the fourteenth-century version in **StM**, perfect longs in the original thirteenth-century notation were erroneously signified as longs (though they should have been written as perfect breves). This is clear evidence that the process of updating the notation depended on a written exemplar, since had the piece been sung or replicated from memory within

---

55 Adam's *opera omina* has a section devoted to polyphonic, but not monophonic, rondeaux.
56 On the date and provenance of **Ivrea**, see Kügle 2019.
57 See Thomas 1985, vol. 3, ii and 26. This identification was also noted and discussed in Saltzstein 2008, 184–86. See also Saltzstein 2019b, 358–59, where she proposes that this tenor was a quotation of the refrain from Adam's *Jeu*.
58 See the discussion of this phenomenon in Maw 2004, esp. 46–48. See also Bent 2015, 40–41.
59 Leach 2011; see also Stenzl 1970.

the conventions of the newer notational framework, such a counter-intuitive error would be unlikely.

In the immediate context of **Ivrea**, there was no attempt to adjust the rhythmic values of the two thirteenth-century motets recorded elsewhere in this source: *Leis l'ormelle/Main se leva/JE NE CHAINDRAI* and *Clap, clap, par un matin/Sus Robin/[TENOR]*.[60] These pieces, which were evidently copied from an older exemplar in thirteenth-century notation, simply maintained their original longs and breves. By contrast, Adam's refrain was translated, and very successfully, into shorter note values in *Prenes l'abre*. It is hard to say how and why Adam's refrain was known and selected for use as the tenor of only the initial section of a fourteenth-century polyphonic virelai, uniquely recorded in **Ivrea** and indeed the only virelai contained in this source. But the fact of the refrain's (successful) notational translation could suggest that it was known first-hand, either from Adam's *Jeu* or his hypothetical rondeau. That is, the refrain was recalled and adopted in *Prenes l'abre* – and quite naturally notated in the new breves and semibreves that corresponded to its established tempo – because it was still in musical memory and/or oral circulation. Adam's version of the refrain may have suggested itself as a tenor here, precisely because its own unusual ABB′ form – with B sections leading alternate open and closed endings – recalled that of a typical virelai.

If the internal virelai characteristics of Adam's *He resveille toi* refrain were the impetus for its adoption in *Prenes l'abre*, this would argue against an alternative hypothesis: that awareness of the refrain as polyphonic tenor in the late thirteenth-century motet repertoire caused it to preserve the same function in the fourteenth century.[61] In this regard, it is notable too that the rondeau form which characterises the thirteenth-century HE RESVEILLE TOI tenor is not exploited in *Prenes l'abre*. Yet whether Adam's refrain was known from motet, *Jeu*, rondeau, or several of these contexts, it remained of sufficient interest to feature as the accompaniment for the start of a fourteenth-century polyphonic virelai. That this refrain was used at all, and moreover assumed within

---

60 See the final rows of Table 5.1 for concordances.

61 Diergarten 2014, 149–53, argues that *Prenes l'abre* combines techniques of motet and song composition, underlining the fact that the version of Adam's refrain in *Prenes l'abre* shares its final (undecorated) cadence with the tenor of the **Mo 7** motet, in contrast to the monophonic version of the refrain in Adam's *Jeu* (see the comparative transcription at 151). Although the motet and virelai tenors share their final cadence, the fact remains that the first A section and the start of the first B section depart from the motet *and* refrain versions in the tenor of *Prenes l'abre*. Moreover, the omission of the refrain's antepenultimate decorative passing note – which is written out in the copy of the *Jeu* in **Ha**, but shown only as a plica in **Méjanes** – could plausibly have occurred independently in both polyphonic contexts, in order to simplify the melodic profile of the lowest voice in approach to a final cadence and/ or to mirror the rhythmic profile of the preceding B material.

Example 1.9 Adam de la Halle, polyphonic rondeau *Fi, mari*, **Ha**, fol. 33r–v

the new rhythmic idiom of its song context, is a significant testament to the circulation – written, oral, or a combination of both – and longevity of Adam's particular version of *He resveille toi*.

Quoting Adam's Polyphonic Rondeaux: Fi, mari

The remaining anonymous motets with links to Adam in fascicle 7 make reference to his polyphonic rondeaux, known from his corpus in **Ha**. The first of these motets, *Dame bele/Fi, mari/NUS N'IERT JA JOLIS*, quotes Adam polyphonically. This motet was copied directly after *En mai/L'autre jour/HE RESVEILLE TOI* in **Reg**, the only known source beyond **Mo** 7 to preserve either of these compositions. Just like Adam's own motet *Aucun/A Dieu/SUPER TE*, the opening of *Dame bele/Fi, mari/NUS N'IERT JA JOLIS* closely resembles, in all three voices, the music of a polyphonic rondeau by Adam, *Fi, mari*, whose accompanying refrain text is present in the motetus. Example 1.9 gives Adam's rondeau *Fi, mari* for comparison with the motet *Dame bele/Fi, mari/NUS N'IERT JA JOLIS*, shown in Example 1.10. As in *Aucun/A Dieu/SUPER TE*, it seems that the creator of *Dame bele/Fi, mari/NUS N'IERT JA JOLIS* modelled this motet polyphonically on a three-voice rondeau by Adam, choosing a suitable tenor quotation to replicate the melodic contour of the lowest voice of Adam's *Fi, mari* (variants in the lowest voices that result in harmonic differences are marked by boxes).

In *Dame bele/Fi, mari/NUS N'IERT JA JOLIS*, the tenor apparently quotes not a liturgical plainchant but rather the text and (presumably) the melody of the rondeau *Nus n'iert ja jolis*. Outside the tenor voice of *Dame bele/Fi, mari/NUS N'IERT JA JOLIS*, this rondeau survives uniquely in the manuscript **PaB**, a source designed to accommodate the music of three-voice rondeaux but in which staves and notation were never entered.[62] **PaB** provides the complete text of the polyphonic rondeau *Nus n'iert ja jolis*, but it can only be presumed – albeit plausibly – that the missing music of the middle voice of this polyphonic rondeau matched the tenor of *Dame bele/Fi, mari/NUS N'IERT JA JOLIS*.[63] As in the relationship between *Aucun/A Dieu/ SUPER TE* and its rondeau source, the triplum voices in *Fi mari* and *Dame bele/Fi, mari/NUS N'IERT JA JOLIS* are the most divergent, but they have the same musical incipit, whose continuation also shares details of melodic contour and rhythmic outline, as well as similar explicits (marked by dashed boxes in Example 1.9). In their presentation of the refrain vdB 746, the middle voices of the two compositions are musically and textually identical.[64] And the two lowest voices begin identically before diverging slightly: the motet tenor has a different pitch at the end of perfection 3, and it is shorter than the lowest voice of Adam's rondeau, effecting the same final G – F cadence progression but in a different rhythm at an earlier point in the refrain melody.[65]

Though slight, such musical divergences support the argument that the motet did not simply reproduce, and then retext, the lowest voice of Adam's *Fi, mari*. The status of the NUS N'IERT JA JOLIS tenor as a quotation – of another genuine rondeau text and melody – is corroborated also by the scrupulous preservation and structural importance of its rondeau form (indicated by circled letters in Example 1.10), presented in full in the motet. Furthermore, the first return of the A music of the tenor's rondeau with its accompanying refrain text 'nus n'iert ja jolis' (tenor text line 4, at perfections 9–11) is matched by a reprise of the A music of the motetus's rondeau refrain (indicated by a boxed letter and marked by a dashed box in Example 1.10).

---

62 See **PaB**, fol. 79v. On **PaB**, see Everist 1996, 61–69. Everist considers **PaB** to be 'contemporary' (61) with **Ha**.

63 The middle voice of a thirteenth-century polyphonic rondeau can be considered its melody; see Everist 2019, 337. It is always the middle voices of such rondeaux that have concordances with monophonic rondeaux in other sources, and quotations of refrain melodies from polyphonic rondeaux in this period invariably match their middle voices.

64 Like vdB 496 (see n. 32), vdB 746 also appears, with music, in two copies of *Renart le nouvel*, this time in **Renart F** and in **Ha**. As is typical of refrains that appear on multiple occasions in **Ha**, the version of the refrain in *Renart le nouvel* matches exactly that in the rondeau by Adam found earlier in the same manuscript. **Renart F**, however, presents a different refrain melody.

65 While it could be argued that the tenor was altered to create the overlapping phrase structure characteristic of motets, such independence of motetus and tenor phrasing was not enforced in *Aucun/A Dieu/SUPER TE*, where these voices cadence together at the presentation of the rondeau refrain's A material.

Example 1.10 Motet *Dame bele/Fi, mari/NUS N'IERT JA JOLIS*, **Mo** 7, fols. 300v–301r

The motetus's refrain melody is accompanied by a line of text – line 4, 'qui me sert et nuit et jour' – that also appears later in Adam's *Fi, mari* rondeau (as line 5, accompanying the same A music and marked by a dashed box in Example 1.9). The relationship between *Dame bele/Fi, mari/NUS N'IERT*

JA JOLIS and Adam's *Fi, mari* rondeau thus extends beyond their shared refrain.[66] That an additional textual connection between the two compositions occurs at a structurally significant moment in *Dame bele/Fi, mari/ NUS N'IERT JA JOLIS*, motivated by the independent rondeau form of the tenor, arguably underlines the status of the line 'qui me sert et nuit et jour' as a quotation in the motet. It is harder to explain why Adam would borrow just one additional line of a motet text for the fifth line of his rondeau.[67] In this case, *Dame bele/Fi, mari/NUS N'IERT JA JOLIS* seems to be in homage to Adam, not only in quoting his polyphonic rondeau in conjunction with a rondeau tenor melody, but possibly also in copying his technique of polyphonic refrain quotation, achieved here by the very same means – the selection of a pre-existing tenor melody with a similar profile to that of the lowest voice of Adam's rondeau – as in Adam's *Aucun/A Dieu/SUPER TE*.

Two Quotations of Adam's Rondeau Refrain 'He, Dieus, quant verrai'

The case for quotation (or for polyphonic quotation) of Adam is not so clear-cut in two further fascicle 7 motets that contain the music and text of the refrain of Adam's rondeau *He, Dieus, quant verrai* (vdB 823; see Example 1.11). Poetically, this refrain is quite generic, such that similar but not identical instantiations of its text are found – without melodies – across the three manuscript sources of the *Roman de la violette*.[68] In this context, it is striking that two independent motets in fascicle 7 contain this same refrain, and in versions that are poetically and musically identical with the middle voice of Adam's rondeau. The melodic stability of '*He, Dieus, quant verrai*' across all three extant versions is remarkable, since refrains are otherwise apt to vary in precisely the kinds of

---

66 Ludwig 1978, 436, noted the appearance of the additional line of text from Adam's rondeau in *Dame bele/Fi, mari/NUS N'IERT JA JOLIS* in conjunction with the beginning of the refrain melody. This has subsequently been noted only in Ibos-Augé 2019, 261–62. This is also the case in the Adam's motet *Aucun/A Dieu/SUPER TE*, where poetic material beyond Adam's quoted rondeau refrain is incorporated in the motetus text, with some adjustments. See the discussion in Huot 1987b, 157; Ibos-Augé 2019, 266–67.

67 Syllable count was not the determining factor, since lines 3 and 6 of the motetus text are also of the seven syllables required for the rondeau's A material. It would be surprising had Adam selected only lines 1, 2, and 4 of the motetus, rather than simply appropriating lines 1–4 in their entirety.

68 See the transcription of these texts in Anne Ibos-Augé, *REFRAIN: Musique, poésie, citation: le refrain au moyen âge/Music, Poetry, Citation: The Medieval Refrain*, http://refrain. ac.uk/view/abstract_item/823.html (accessed 25 June 2020).

Example 1.11 Adam de la Halle, refrain of polyphonic rondeau *He, Dieus, quant verrai*, **Ha**, fol. 34r

decorative details that remain entirely stable here. The final motet of fascicle 7 proper, *Bien met amours/Dame, alegies ma grevance/APERIS*, presents Adam's rondeau refrain internally, as the penultimate phrase of the triplum voice (see Example 1.12).[69] It is difficult to argue for any polyphonic quotation in this motet, but the overall outline of the motet tenor is quite similar to the lowest voice of Adam's rondeau, as is the wider harmonic context of the refrain melody (provided, respectively, by the upper voice of the rondeau and the motetus: shared pitches are marked by dashed boxes in Examples 1.11 and 1.12).

Similarly, the motetus of *Theotheca, virgo geratica/Las, pour qoi/ QUI PRANDOIT* – the unique and final motet of **Mo** 7's second supplement – concludes with another strikingly exact match for the melody and text of the same rondeau refrain (see Example 1.13).[70] Once again, the refrain appears here over a tenor contour and accompanied by a triplum that provides a broadly similar harmonic context to both *Bien met amours/Dame, alegies ma grevance/APERIS* and Adam's rondeau *He, Dieus, quant verrai* (shared pitches marked by dashed boxes in Example 1.13). Yet it is difficult to argue that any direct polyphonic modelling or quotation is at work. In both of these motets, it seems that tenors were not expressly selected to accommodate polyphonic quotations of Adam's rondeau refrain, but rather that a similarity of tenor contour to that of

---

69 Walker 1982, 322 identified the established plainchant motet tenor APERIS (M 69) as the basis of this motet, preserved in full only in **Mo** 7 but whose motetus incipit is also listed in **Bes**. The tenor voice is wrongly labelled in **Mo** as 'A Paris', as if it were a vernacular song about Paris (of the kind discussed in Chapter 3).
70 See Butterfield 2002, 282.

Example 1.12 Refrain 'He, Dieus, quant verrai' in *Bien met amours/Dame, alegies ma grevance/ APERIS*, **Mo** 7, fol. 333v, perfections 52–61

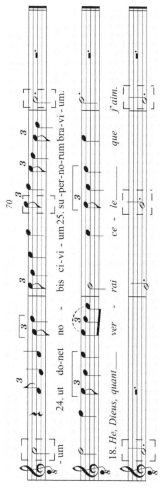

Example 1.13 Refrain 'He, Dieus, quant verrai' in *Theotheca, virgo geratica/Las, pour qoi/QUI PRANDOIT*, **Mo 7**, fol. 349v, perfections 67–72

the lowest voice of Adam's polyphonic rondeau may have prompted the quotation of his refrain melody, which in turn prompted or lent itself to a similar harmonisation (by intervals of a fifth, unison, or octave) in the new motet context. The fact that this same refrain is found, identically, in two different motets near the end of fascicle 7 underlines the refrain's status as a genuine quotation in the context of this motet collection and strengthens the possibility that this text and melody carried with it the association of Adam's authorship. Possibly, the later addition of *Theotheca, virgo geratica/Las, pour qoi/QUI PRANDOIT* in fascicle 7's second supplement was in response not only to other quotations of Adam's rondeau refrains earlier in this fascicle but also specifically to the appearance of '*He, Dieus, quant verrai*' in *Bien met amours/Dame, alegies ma grevance/APERIS*.

Motets Quoting Adam's Motets: *Se je sui/Jolietement/OMNES*

The single example in **Mo** fascicle 8 of a motet linked to Adam, the unicum *Se je sui/Jolietement/OMNES*, differs from all those discussed previously in that it makes direct reference not to a rondeau or a refrain by Adam but to a motet: his widely transmitted and self-referential *Entre Adam/Chief bien seans/APTATUR*. *Se je sui/Jolietement/OMNES* quotes, at the close of its triplum voice, the text and music (transposed up a fifth) of the incipit of Adam's motetus 'Chief bien seans' (marked by a box in Example 1.14). Such quotation, not of a conventional refrain but rather of the incipit of a motet voice, is remarkable.[71] Ibos-Augé has demonstrated that the quotation in motets of musico-poetic snippets from other motets is a relatively rare and late thirteenth-century phenomenon.[72] It usually occurs in motet tripla, which typically quote other motet triplum incipits, and is most prevalent among compositions in **Mo**'s final fascicles.

Adam's motetus incipit 'Chief bien seans' is effectively placed in quotation marks – poetically and musically – at the end of the triplum *Se je sui*. This first-person text opens with the poet's declaration that he is inspired to sing by the beauty and goodness of his lady, which he goes on to describe. The triplum

---

71 Ibos-Augé 2019, 265, emphasises that 'Chief biean seans' is not a refrain, but rather a 'fragment' quoted in homage to Adam.

72 Ibos-Augé 2018a. Ibos-Augé identifies five examples of motets that quote motets. Two of these pieces – *Se je sui/Jolietement/OMNES* and *Mout me fu grief/Robin m'aime/PORTARE* – involve quotations of Adam. Indeed, Adam's quotation of the refrain vdB 1473 in *Dame/Dieus, comment/OMNES* in the same harmonic context as it is found in *Tant me fait/Tout li cuers/OMNES* discussed earlier, could be considered a further example of a (polyphonic) quotation of a motet, as well as of a refrain.

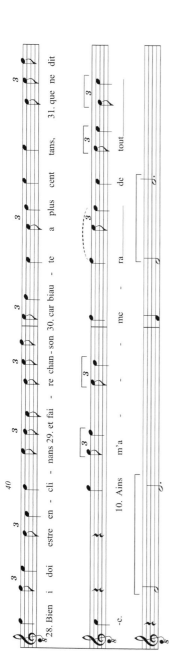

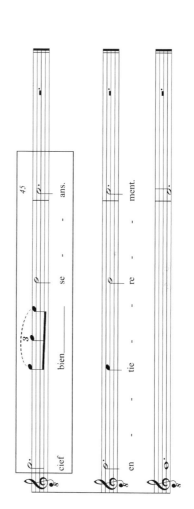

Example 1.14 Adam's incipit 'Chief bien seans' in *Se je sui/Jolietement/OMNES*, **Mo** 8, fol. 365v, perfections 39–46

closes by returning to the theme of song-making that is inspired by love, stating that (see Example 1.14): 'I must indeed be serviceable/and make a song/because [her] beauty is a hundred times more/than is expressed by "A shapely head"'. The poet, therefore, explicitly compares his own song to Adam's, asserting his superiority of musical and poetic expression over Adam's more old-fashioned, typical, and straightforwardly descriptive love song. There is a clear musical contrast between the quickly declaimed text of *Se je sui* – which is entirely syllabic and precedes exclusively in semibreves and breves – and the noticeably slower-moving profile of its final quotation from Adam. The rhythmic values of this closing quotation shift, for the first time in *Se je sui*, to breves and longs.[73] The quotation's semibreves are distinguished by the fact that they are purely decorative rather than syllabic, representing the first and only melisma of the entire triplum. Musically therefore, *Se je sui* is distinctly modern – with its pairs and trios of texted semibreves – by comparison with Adam's *Chief bien seans* motetus. The **Mo** 8 triplum is in a faster-moving and relentlessly syllabic style that enables, by its self-declared estimation, a more expressive mode of song.

The marked stylistic disjunction between Adam's motetus incipit and the preceding *Se je sui* triplum in **Mo** fascicle 8 stands in contrast to the better-integrated quotations of Adam's refrains and rondeaux within the motets of **Mo** 7. This may reflect a greater temporal and stylistic distance between the quoted material and its fascicle 8 host motet, and/or a particular difference in attitude to Adam in *Se je sui*: one of deliberate new-versus-old contrast and competition rather than straightforward evocation or homage. This stance towards Adam is explored further in Chapter 2, which argues for the quotation of Adam's 'Aucun' incipit at the outset of another stylistically more modern triplum attributed to Petrus de Cruce.

Conclusions

Mo's final fascicles contain a range of motets that engage with Adam's identity as an author in various ways, from three motets by Adam – and which all contain self-references and/or quotations – to those anonymous pieces that quote him: presenting his monophonic rondeaux in full in a motetus or tenor voice, achieving a polyphonic or melody-voice quotation of a three-part rondeau refrain, or closing with a reference to his most famous motetus incipit. It may be that Adam's own evident preoccupation with quotation, polyphonic quotation, and self-quotation inspired a similar response to his work in others. Indeed, it could have been Adam's attempts to recreate the polyphonic contexts of his rondeaux in his motets that opened up not only the possibility of multi-voiced

---

73 This invites comparison with the quotation in Machaut's ballade no. 12, *Pour ce que tous*, of the refrain of Denis le Grant's chace *Se je chant* (also the opening text of the motetus of **Mo** 7, no. 277), on which see Kügle 1997a, 158–62. In Machaut's ballade, the *Se je chant* quotation is similarly set apart by its longer note values.

quotation but also the types of sources from which quotations might be drawn, not just refrains and songs but three-voice rondeaux and motets themselves. Adam's role in such practices may be artificially amplified by the survival of his unusual author corpus, which uniquely allows quotations of him to be perceived within unattributed polyphonic compositions. Nevertheless, these anonymous polyphonic compositions themselves often reveal an even broader circulation and longevity of Adam's materials than extant written sources attest: the possible existence of a lost monophonic rondeau *He resveille toi*, for instance, and the endurance of this refrain well into the fourteenth century.

Adam's output and authorship, then, was apparently distinctive and long-lived within cultures of polyphonic composition. Although several of his quoted rondeau refrains are conventional, strongly rooted within existing refrain traditions, and even generic, they nonetheless circulated in a fixed and individual version that was particular to Adam. In the case of *He resveille toi*, a refrain that Adam himself borrowed, it was his specific and unusual tripartite form of this refrain that became predominant. Works by and quoting Adam are noticeably concentrated in **Mo** fascicle 7, and while this could indicate a certain bias of the codex's compilers, it might equally reflect **Mo** 7's status as the most substantive surviving witness to this particular layer of the thirteenth-century motet repertoire. This raises broader questions, explored further in Chapters 2 and 3, as to why Adam was of such interest in the creative context now best represented by **Mo** 7: what were these unknown composers' attitudes towards Adam and the intentions behind their references to his works? The quotation of Adam may merely have been part of a general interest in quotational play at which Adam himself was so adept, or it could have represented a kind of homage, and in the case of *Se je sui* in the spirit of competition, invoking an older composer in order to highlight the innovative superiority of a newer style.

2 Adam and Petrus de Cruce

The 'Aucun . . .' Opening and Questions of Chronology

A Shared Incipit

Adam de la Halle's motet *Aucun se sont loe/A Dieu commant/SUPER TE* opens with a polyphonic self-quotation. As demonstrated in the preceding chapter, Adam's motetus begins by quoting the refrain text and melody of his three-voice rondeau *A Dieu commant*, while the surrounding triplum and tenor voices recreate the harmonic context of the original rondeau (see Examples 1.1 and 1.2). Notwithstanding accommodations to the new generic context of the motet – a plainchant tenor quotation and an independently texted and fast-moving triplum – *Aucun/A Dieu/SUPER TE* gives a strong aural impression of Adam's rondeau source. Arguably, this initial self-quotation carries an equally strong impression of Adam's identity as the motet's creator.

The very beginning of Adam's motet triplum is itself replicated at the outset of the triplum of another motet, *Aucun ont trouve/Lonc tens/ ANNUN[TIANTES]*, attributed to Petrus de Cruce and recorded in **Mo** 7 and in **Tu** (see Example 2.1, which reproduces dots of division in the original notation in order to clarify breve units). Fascicle 7 of **Mo** begins with two motets that are – as discussed in detail in Chapter 4 – ascribed to Petrus in theoretical treatises, where they exemplify the division of a perfect breve into more than three semibreves. The first motet of the fascicle, *S'amour eust/Au renouveler/ECCE*, is attributed to Petrus only by the fourteenth-century theorist known as Jacobus.[1] But a host of additional theorists cite the triplum incipit of **Mo** 7's second motet, *Aucun ont trouve/Lonc tens/ANNUN[TIANTES]*, and name Petrus as its creator.[2] The first five notes of Petrus's *Aucun ont*

---

1 See Bent 2015, 21–27.
2 On theoretical citations of *Aucun ont trouve* and their attributions, see Bent 2015, 27–32; Catalunya 2018, 420–22. There is an additional unattributed citation of this triplum incipit in the recently discovered treatise in the Free Library of Philadelphia, Lewis E 39, fol. 1r–v (on fol. 1r).

DOI: 10.4324/9781003259282-3

Example 2.1 'Aucun' motet incipits

trouve triplum are an exact musical match for the opening of Adam's *Aucun se sont loe* (marked by boxes in Example 2.1). The two tripla are rhythmically and melodically identical, and at the same pitch level (beginning on f). Shared poetic elements are marked in bold in Example 2.1: the opening word 'Aucun', the internal '-e' rhyme ('loe'/'trouve'), and the initial conjunction 'but' ('mais'/'mes'). The principal divergence in these 'Aucun' incipits is that where Adam's three-semibreve group is melismatic (carrying the single syllable 'se'), Petrus's is syllabic (setting the three syllables 'ont trouve').

This musically identical triplum incipit, in conjunction with the shared opening text incipit 'Aucun', cannot be pure coincidence. The melodic profile of the triplum is not strikingly distinctive in the wider context of **Mo** 7 and 8; nevertheless just these two motets have it in common. The opening word 'Aucun' is more prevalent in these fascicles where it appears in two further motets (see Example 2.1). One – *Aucuns vont souvent/Amor, qui cor vulnerat/KYRIE ELEYSON* (**Mo** no. 264, also found in **Tu**) – directly follows Adam's *Aucun se sont loe* in fascicle 7, while the other is a unicum in fascicle 8 (*Aucun, qui ne sevent/Iure tuis/[VIRGO] MARIA*, no. 317). Both of these motets with 'Aucun' tripla divide their breve into as many as six syllabic semibreves, inviting comparison with Petrus's *Aucun ont trouve* (in which there is also one occurrence of a seven-semibreve group). Musically, the two incipits share some details of texting and contour with Petrus's and Adam's, but not to a degree that suggests direct quotation or modelling: both open with a repeated semibreve pitch for the two syllables of 'Aucun' (here a in both cases) and then fall a tone (to G), which initiates a syllabic three-semibreve group in *Aucun, qui ne sevent/Iure tuis/[VIRGO] MARIA* (see Example 2.1). Poetically, all four **Mo** 7 and 8 motets exploit the opening 'Aucun' to the same rhetorical end. The attitude to love of 'some' who remain abstract is briefly characterised at the outset, as a basis to launch an extended and contrasting and personal reflection. Only Adam's triplum espouses a negative attitude to love; although 'Some have praised love', he blames it for pain and advises against it. In Petrus's *Aucun ont trouve* (as discussed further later), love is – by contrast – a positive inspiration to sing in a way that is unlike 'some' who 'compose out of habit'. Both *Aucuns vont souvent* and *Aucun, qui ne sevent servir amour* are a defence of love against 'some' who speak ill of it.

'Aucun' was a relatively common first word for monophonic songs, employed in ten instances in the trouvère repertoire, of which five begin (unlike any extant motets) with the more extended form 'Aucune gent' ('some people').[3] Yet it was not a standard word among refrain openings or refrain lexis in general, and within the motet repertoire the incipit is found in only one

---

3   See the list of 'Aucun' incipits in Raynaud-Spanke 1980, 306.

composition outside the four related tripla concentrated in **Mo** 7 and 8.[4] This is the two-voice *Aucuns m'ont par lour envie/ANGELUS* recorded in **W2** and in **N**, which circulated widely in six further manuscript sources (receiving several contrafactum texts and added tripla) as well as in theoretical treatises.[5] The motet was copied twice, in two different versions, in **Mo**. It appears in fascicle 5, with the 'Aucun' motetus incipit (no. 128, *J'ai si bien/Aucun m'ont/ANGE-LUS*), and with alternative texts and a different triplum with pairs of syllabic semibreves in fascicle 3 (no. 39, *Povre secors/Gaude chorus/ANGLEUS*). Once again, this 'Aucun' incipit (marked by a dashed box in Example 2.1) has a similar melodic shape to that of Adam and Petrus, although transposed down a fifth (to start on c) and in the slower-moving second rhythmic mode. Poetically, the opening function of 'Aucun' is shared with many of the songs beginning 'Aucun', but differs from the more abstract philosophical usage in the **Mo** 7 and 8 motets. This motetus asserts that 'Some' (acting out of envy, as in **Mo** 7, no. 264) have made false accusations: it is not love, but rather the first-person narrator that has been denounced, and he seeks to defend himself, such that the 'aucun' text is in an active, accusatory mode.

The brief 'Aucun' incipit shared by Adam and Petrus clearly, then, did not come out of nowhere. It adopted an established poetic gesture within monophonic songs and possibly even mimicked the melody associated with the much-reworked *Aucuns m'ont/ANGELUS* motet. Nevertheless, the exact match between the beginning of Adam and Petrus's tripla stands out in the context of other beginnings that are only broadly similar. And this raises the question as to who is alluding to whom. In terms of relative dissemination, each motet survives in just one source beyond **Mo** 7. Petrus's *Aucun ont trouve/Lonc tens/ANNUN[TIANTES]* is the second of the two motets attributed to him that open **Mo** 7, but this is not the case in **Tu**, where these two motets by Petrus are separated and not so significantly positioned.[6] Conversely, Adam's *Aucun se sont loe/A Dieu commant/SUPER TE* opens his motet corpus in **Ha**, but it is not obviously privileged in **Mo** 7. Unlike Adam's, Petrus's incipit achieved notable fame in music theory treatises, and was probably responsible for the adoption of the 'Aucun' text opening in two further tripla in the same multi-note style. Garbled theoretical citations of *Aucun ont trouve*, as well as confusion among theorists concerning the maximum number of semibreves used in this motet, underline Margaret Bent's view that Petrus's incipit took on a theoretical life of its own, somewhat divorced from the reality of the motet in practice.[7]

---

4 'Aucun' opens just one refrain (vdB 194) and is found internally in just one other (vdB 441).
5 Gennrich 1957, no. 263. Like *Aucun ont trouve*, this motet incipit was widely used as a theoretical example, although crucially with the alternative motetus text *Gaude chorus omnium*.
6 This was also emphasised by Bent 2015, 25.
7 On the independence of the theoretical citations from musical practice, see Bent 2015, 30–32.

Placing Adam, Franco, and Petrus

On purely stylistic grounds, and based on the scattered biographical details for both Adam and Petrus, Adam seems to have been the older of the two composers. Petrus, in his use of more than three semibreves within the time of a perfect breve, exceeds the theoretical definitions of the breve by Lambertus and by Franco, in his definitive and widely circulated *Ars cantus mensurabilis musicae*.[8] Moreover, Petrus's two attributed motets pursue a radically rhythmically stratified style, first seen in **Mo** 7, in which slow-moving tenors support multi-note and syllabic tripla. Adam's motets, on the other hand, are (as discussed in Chapter 1) stylistically more akin to the latest works in **Mo**'s old corpus, and he never exceeds the division of the breve into three.[9] Petrus was surely younger than Franco, whose art – as Jacobus tells us – he 'followed'.[10] Adam, on the other hand, was probably of the same or an earlier generation to Franco and, on the basis of his surviving works, was musically more conservative than either Franco or Petrus.[11]

Very little is known abut Franco's identity, let alone the details of his life, but a date of c.1280, as established by Jeremy Yudkin, is now accepted for his *Ars cantus*.[12] This hinges on a colophon, which provides a secure 1279 date for the treatise of the Parisian theorist known as the St Emmeram Anonymous, who models his work on Johannes de Garlandia's and engages (combatively) with concepts espoused in Parisian treatises first by Lambertus and then by Franco. These concepts were known to the St Emmeram Anonymous only from Lambertus, however, as Franco is not mentioned in his 1279 treatise. By contrast, Franco was named twice by the later theorist Anonymous IV, writing probably in the mid-1280s.[13] A date of c.1280 for Franco's treatise – subsequent but in close proximity to those of Lambertus and the St Emmeram anonymous – is in line with the conventional view

---

8 See Grier 2021, 85–86, on the importance of Lambertus – whose treatise predates Franco's – in the tripartite codification of the breve.

9 The only instance in which Adam's music is at odds with Franco's theory occurs in his polyphonic rondeau *Or est baiars*, where a duplex long is imperfected by a breve, on which see Maw 2020, 499; Maw 2006, 51–55. I believe that this was a performative effect, which proved problematic to express in conventional notation.

10 See the edition and translation of this passage of Jacobus's *Speculum musicae* in Bent 2015, 22–24. As discussed in Zayaruznaya 2020, 123, Robertus de Handlo (whose treatise is dated to 1326) clearly positions Petrus after Franco.

11 With respect to Franco's theory, Adam's motets are also conservative, because they never chain pairs and trios of texted semibreves and thus never require Franco's clarificatory dots of division.

12 See Yudkin 1982, 232–38. See also Grier 2021, 64–65 and 85.

13 On the (relative) date of Anonymous IV, see Grier 2021, 65 and 85. See also Wegman 2015, 714–15.

that Petrus 'flourished' in the 1290s.[14] This view fits in turn, and to some extent depends on, the accepted 1290s date of **Mo** fascicle 7 – for which this monograph assembles additional evidence – in which Petrus's attributed works and heavily syllabic tripla are present for the first time, and also in much greater number than in the later eighth fascicle.[15]

There are two firm pieces of documentary evidence relating to Petrus's life: a 'Magister Petrus de Cruce de Ambianis' stayed at the King's castle in Paris in 1298, where he was paid to compose a rhymed plainchant Office for St Louis, and a 'Maistres Pierre de le crois' was in the household of the Bishop of Amiens in 1301–2, where he bequeathed to the Cathedral a book of polyphony (possibly of motets, since it opened with a *Deus in adiutorium*) that had been received by 1347.[16] However long Petrus actually lived and whatever his subsequent compositional activity, he achieved greatest and lasting notoriety for the multi-semibreve motets singled out by later theorists. By the 1290s, Franco and – as argued later in the chapter – Adam had the status of respected masters. Petrus, on the other hand, could still have been a relatively young man when his motets were selected, possibly with the status of cutting-edge compositions, to open **Mo**'s seventh fascicle.

Orientating Adam and Dating *Aucun se sont loe/A Dieu commant/SUPER TE*

Secure dates within the evidence surrounding Adam are two decades earlier than those for Petrus. Adam is mentioned in the *Congé* by Baude Fastoul, composed in the year of his death, 1272; Adam's *jeux-partis* make explicit his youth relative to Jehan Bretel, with whom he debated before Bretel's death, also in 1272; and Adam's *Jeu d'Adam ou de la feuilee* post-dates the second Council of Lyon in 1276.[17] Narratives hypothesised on the basis of

14 See Ernest H. Sanders and Peter M. Lefferts, 'Petrus de Cruce', *Grove Music Online* (accessed 15 Aug. 2020), https://doi.org/10.1093/gmo/9781561592630.article.21491.

15 Zayaruznaya 2020, 122–25, challenges Petrus's consignment principally to the 1290s as part of her claim that the seventh book of Jacobus's *Speculum musicae*, completed after Petrus's death, was written not in the 1330s (as has long been thought) but rather in the 1350s. On the contrary, the idea that the techniques and style associated with Petrus – which does not speak for the length of Petrus's own life – flourished for a relatively brief period remains plausible, given the generally modest circulation of Petrus's works (in **Mo** 7 and **Tu**) and the presence of only three works with tripla exceeding the division of the breve into three in **Mo** 8.

16 See the summary of Petrus's biography in Bent 2015, 32–34. See also Zayaruznaya 2020, 122–25; Johnson 1991, 460–95. On *Deus in adiutorium* as an opening for motet collections, see Maschke 2018.

17 See the summary of chronological markers for Adam in Saltzstein 2019, 2–10. See also Ibos-Augé 2018b, 230–33.

Adam's fictional but apparently autobiographical works remain less certain. The *Jeu d'Adam* expresses, for instance, a desire to return to studies in Paris. A farewell to Arras in Adam's *Congé* has also been taken as indication that he departed for Sicily in August 1282, in the service of Robert II, Count of Artois and his uncle Charles of Anjou, the subject of Adam's incomplete *Le Roi de Sezile*.[18] It is probable that Adam did not die in Arras, since his name is absent from the city's famous necrology.[19] And an explicit in a copy of the *Roman de Troie* compiled by a certain Jehanes Madot before 1289 claims that Adans li Boscus was his uncle, who had left Arras, and was now dead.[20] The *Jeu du pelerin*, uniquely recorded in **Ha** as a prequel to Adam's *Jeu de Robin et Marion*, reports in a light and comic tone that Adam was in Apulia and that he died and was buried there.[21] Though a work of fiction, and a comic one at that, this would corroborate the theory that Adam was dead before the copying of **Ha** in the 1290s.[22]

Adam's motet *Aucun/A Dieu/SUPER TE* has previously been dated precisely to the year 1269. Recent citations of this dating refer to a fiscal scandal involving the 'devaluation' of the *tournois* coin in 1269, which Adam's motetus text states has 'blinded counts and kings': 'gros tournois ont avugle

18 See Symes 2007, 238, who suggests that Adam departed for Italy in August 1282. See also Robert Falck, 'Adam de la Halle', *Grove Music Online* (accessed 27 Mar. 2020), https://doi.org/10.1093/gmo/9781561592630.article.00163, who emphasises Robert II's departure for Italy in 1283.
19 The death of a 'Bochu maistre Henri', named in Baude Fastoul's *Congé* and Adam's own *Jeu d'Adam* as Adam's father, is recorded in the necrology. Henri's death seems to have occurred in 1290, after the death date commonly accepted for his son Adam. On the necrology, see Berger 1963–70, see also Falck, 'Adam de la Halle'.
20 I say before 1289 because the evidence is contradictory. Ibos-Augé 2018b, 233, notes that this manuscript is itself dated to 2 February 1289. Yet Falck, 'Adam de la Halle', and Symes 2019, 29, have dated Madot's testimony by the fact that – according to the Arras necrology – Madot himself died in 1288. It seems unlikely that Adam's nephew should die in the late 1280s, around the same time as Adam himself, who apparently died young and pre-deceased his own father. Ibos-Augé's evidence suggests that the Jehan Madot in the necrology is not the same as Adam's self-declared nephew.
21 Falck, 'Adam de la Halle', does not discuss the *Jeu du pelerin*. Symes 2019, 28–32, places some weight on this evidence, however, committed to the hypothesis that Adam died in Italy at the end of the 1280s and that **Ha** was a posthumous compilation. Her views are broadly accepted in Saltzstein 2019a, 9–10.
22 Falck, 'Adam de la Halle', leaves open the possibility that Adam could have been the 'maistre Adam le Boscu' included in a list of minstrels engaged in 1306 for the coronation of Edward II in 1307. Symes 2019, 30, believes that Adam would have been too old and paid too little to be this musician. **Ha** contains basically everything attributed to Adam, such that if he had lived for at least another decade – until after 1307 – it would seem that he produced nothing further in these years.

contes et rois'.[23] This misrepresents a hypothesis first put forward in Henri Guy's 1898 essays on Adam's life and works. Guy posits that Adam's mote-tus, whose framing refrain speaks also of 'sighing in a strange land', refers to an exile in Douai.[24] He goes to considerable lengths to establish the date of this exile, which he attributes to financial troubles in Arras, in 1269.[25] The story of Adam's exile in Douai has now been shown to be erroneous, based on a misinterpretation of a line in Baude Fastoul's *Congé*.[26] Moreover Guy, and later Yvonne Rokseth, do not refer to a specific devaluation of the *tournois* coin, but rather to raised taxes and fraud in Arras in general.[27] Such financial upheaval was, however, a recurring theme in late thirteenth-century Artois and cannot be pinned down to a single decade.[28] Tax fraud is discussed at length in several of the *Chansons et dits* from Arras preserved in **N** and now dated by Roger Berger in the years 1260–65, on the basis of the numerous individuals named in the texts.[29] Carol Symes places Adam's *Aucun/A Dieu/ SUPER TE* in the 1280s, interpreting the motet's invocation of 'sighing in a strange land' as an indication that Adam was writing it in Italy, after 1282, demonstrating that there was considerable financial unrest in Arras prevalent also in this decade, which would render Adam's motetus text topical.[30]

It is, therefore, problematic to attach chronological significance to Adam's general allusions to the lure of money, as well as to set literal store by his mention of 'sighing in a strange land' – variously interpreted as Douai, Paris, or southern Italy – but which could be merely a poetic pose.[31] In all of this, the key chronological clue in Adam's text has been obscured. Adam does not refer to 'the' *tournois* or to 'many' *tournois*, in which *gros* would be a rather odd choice of adjective to describe quantity, and where we might

23 See Huot 1987b, 157. See also Zingesser 2019, 66.
24 Guy 1898, 87–89.
25 Ibid., 116–28.
26 See Falck, 'Adam de la Halle'. Fastoul's *Congé* refers to a 'Seigneur Henri' and 'Adan, son fil' exiled to Douai. Later in the *Congé* Fastoul bids farewell to a 'maistre' Henri de la Halle and his son Adan. The first reference to 'seigneur', rather than 'maistre', Henri and his son Adam cannot, therefore, be to the de la Halles.
27 Rokseth 1935–39, vol. 4, 78 n. 6, summarises Guy's hypothesis, emphasising the link between the 1269 date and the raising of a tax and resulting tax fraud in Arras. Huot 1987b, 157 (revised in Huot 1997, 49), seems to be the first to refer to the devaluation of the *tour-nois*. This may rest on a reading of the version of Adam's motet text in **Ha**, which is more opaque than that in **Mo** 7: 'gros tournois ont anules ['avugle' in **Mo** 7] contes et rois'.
28 See Billen 2014–15; Small 1993.
29 See Berger 1981, 123–27 (no. II), 175–79 (no. XIII), and 250–58 (no. XXIV).
30 Symes 2007, 203–06.
31 Saltzstein – who does not invoke the 1269 date for Adam's motet text – suggests that this motet expresses Adam's desire to leave Arras for Paris, to resume his studies there. See Saltzstein 2013, 135 and 147.

expect *tournois* to be prefaced by *livres* (i.e. 'Tours pounds' as opposed to the 'Parisian pounds', *livres Parisis*).[32] As several earlier scholars including Guy and Rokseth recognised, the *gros tournois* was itself a specific type of coin.[33] Introduced as part of financial reforms instigated by King Louis IX in the early 1260s, the large silver *gros tournois* coins, worth 12 pennies (*deniers*) were first minted in 1266 and continued to be in circulation into the fourteenth century. This coin was 'much sought after by merchants', and as an innovation new in Adam's lifetime its appearance in a motet text about financial greed seems understandable.[34] It could be tempting to posit that Adam would be more likely to name the *gros tournois* around the time of its invention. Yet the endurance of this coin renders its appearance in *Aucun/A Dieu/SUPER TE* reliable only as a *terminus post quem*: Adam's motet must have been composed after the mid-1260s, but cannot necessarily be placed in this decade.

Adam's Absence From Sources Before 1270: A Retrospective Reputation?

A chronological marker for *Aucun/A Dieu/SUPER TE* serves only to confirm the already accepted view that what is probably Adam's most innovative motet post-dates the mid 1260s. Nevertheless, it offers additional support for current understandings of manuscript chronology, which are themselves revealing in regard to Adam. Adam's works are notably absent from the early layers of the songs or motets in the Artesian Chansonnier de Noailles (**N**), whose copying Gaël Saint-Cricq has recently placed in the decade spanning the late 1260s to 1270s, as well as from **Mo**'s old corpus. Just like **Mo**, the chronology of **N** is layered and complex. As Saint-Cricq has pointed out, the motet collection in **N** 'constitutes a repertory performed, heard, and sometimes composed in Artois between the first decades of the thirteenth century and the 1260s', while 'later collections such as *Tu* or fascicles 7 and 8 in *Mo* show almost no awareness of *N*'.[35] The **N** motets were copied either just before or at the same time as the *Chansons et dits* from Arras (dated by Berger in the early 1260s) and the *Vers de la mort* (dated between 1266 and 1271, and certainly before the death of its author,

---

32 The Artesian song *De canter ne me puis tenir* (RS 1474) – dated in Berger 1981, 123, between 1259 and 1262 – makes reference to 'XX mile livres de Tornois' (see ibid., 125, v. 31).

33 Bastin 1942, 390, drew attention to a mistranslation of *gros tournois* as 'grands tournois', underlining that the *gros tournois* was a coin in its own right. *Gros tournois* has also been misleadingly translated into English as 'great tournaments' in Stakel and Relihan 1985, 86; in Dillon 2012, 157.

34 See Jordan 1979, 208. See also Zingesser 2019 on the prevalence of economic metaphors in thirteenth-century Artesian poetry.

35 Saint-Cricq 2017, xxxii and xix.

Robert le clerc d'Arras, in 1272–73).[36] Adam's absence from this specifically Artesian collection was sufficiently notable that a group of his songs,
with a 'radically different' appearance, was later added at the end of the
manuscript, probably in the early fourteenth century.[37] Yet the fact remains
that neither Adam's monophony nor polyphony was part of a collection of
Artesian materials gathered together, at the earliest in the late 1260s.

Adam's absence from **N** chimes, chronologically, with his absence from
Mo's old corpus, within which the majority of his attributed motets from the
corpus in **Ha** would not have been stylistically out of place. *Entre Adam et
Haniket/Chief bien seans/APTATUR*, old-fashioned by the standards of **Mo** 7,
could – as suggested in the following chapter – have been a deliberately archaic
composition. Yet this cannot account for the absence from **Mo**'s old corpus
of either Adam's *J'os bien m'amie/Je n'os a amie/IN SECULUM* or his *J'ai
ades d'amours/OMNES*, both of which would have been relatively conservative, even in the context of the old corpus. It would seem, therefore, that none
of Adam's motets yet existed or that they were as yet unavailable, unknown, or
insignificant when **Mo** fascicles 2–6 were copied, probably in 1270s Paris.[38]

In terms of Adam's own quotational milieu, he most often quotes his own
rondeaux, but otherwise his motets are connected to those recorded in **Mo**
5, and with motets in this fascicle whose tripla do not feature texted semibreves.[39] As discussed in Chapter 1, Adam quotes in *De ma dame/Dieus,
comment porroie/OMNES* a refrain (vdB 1473) in exactly the same combination with the OMNES tenor as it appears in *Tant me fait/Tout li cuers/
OMNES* (extant as **Mo** 5, no. 115 and in **Ba**). Similarly, the opening '*De ma
dame*' triplum refrain in Adam's motet (vdB 477) also appears in the context
of a fascicle 5 unicum, *Grant solaz/Pleust Diu/NEUMA* (no. 117). Adam's
motets are certainly more like those in **Mo** 5 than in the Artesian motet
collection in **N**, which – even though it must have been copied in Adam's
lifetime – records a noticeably earlier layer of the repertoire. Interestingly,
Adam takes up none of the older Artesian traits of the motets in **N**: he does
not share their interest in Assumption tenors or participate in the quotation
of certain refrains that Saltzstein and Saint-Cricq have localised in Artois.[40]

36 Ibid., xviii.
37 Ibid., xvii–vxiii.
38 If future additional fascicles for **Mo** were already imagined at this stage, it must have been
 decided that Adam's pieces should exclusively belong there.
39 This trend is maintained if Adam's 'Aucun' incipit was indeed related to that in *J'ai si
 bien/Aucun m'ont/ANGELUS*, found in **Mo** fascicle 5 (no. 128) and without a syllabic-
 semibreve triplum (unlike the contrafactum version in **Mo** 3, no. 39).
40 See Saltzstein 2013, 80–113; Saint-Cricq 2017, xxiii–xxxi. Saltzstein 2008, 182–83,
 shows, however, that Adam quotes two refrains with probably Arras heritage in his *Jeu
 de Robin et Marion*. It could also be argued that Adam's interest in a cross-fertilisation
 between motets and rondeaux belongs within an older Artois tradition of the rondeau motet

On the one hand, then, it seems that Adam was not yet widely active or well established as a motet composer around 1270, either in Arras or in Paris.[41] On the other, his motets were apparently created in a context where the motet collection in **N** was recognisably historical, but those in **Mo** fascicle 5 – and not the most cutting-edge of these compositions in terms of texted-semibreve tripla – were still in circulation or living memory. It is tempting to conclude that Adam's motets must have been just too late or not yet of sufficient reputation to enter **Mo**'s old corpus.

Adam's principal period of importance as a motet composer would, then, fall early in any chronological gap between **Mo**'s old corpus and fascicle 7 – that is, in the 1270s or early 1280s – and this would also be in line with the accepted dating for the *Ars cantus* by Franco (roughly his contemporary) and for motets attributed to Petrus (his slightly later successor). This picture is borne out by wider trends in manuscript transmission. Adam's motets feature in **Bes** and **Ba**, two sources that contain pieces from **Mo**'s old corpus as well as from fascicles 7 and 8, but in which relatively earlier layers of the thirteenth-century motet repertoire predominate overall. By contrast, motets associated with Petrus and those which divide the breve units into four or more syllabic semibreves are (with one exception, discussed in detail in Chapter 4) extant exclusively in **Mo** fascicles 7 and 8 and in **Tu** (dated c.1300), collections from which the oldest layers of the repertoire – still evident in **Mo**'s old corpus, **Bes**, or **Ba** – are largely absent.[42] If Adam's motets were already in existence for quite some time before fascicle 7 was copied, this would have given the necessary opportunity for Adam's output to be absorbed and meaningfully invoked by quotation in other compositions recorded in **Mo** 7, as demonstrated in Chapter 1.

The exceptional and concentrated engagement with Adam evident in **Mo** 7 confirms that, even if some of his works were by then more than a decade old, they were still known and still mattered when fascicle 7 was compiled and copied. Indeed, it could be argued that Adam's motets mattered *more* at the time of compilation of **Mo** 7 than at their conception.

(on which see Saint-Cricq 2017, xxix–xxxi). This would, however, constitute a much more general connection to the repertoire of motets recorded in **N** than the specific instances of shared material evident between Adam's motets and those in **Mo** 5.

41 Adam's motets would have been out of keeping in the collection in **N**, even if they were known. However, his songs would not necessarily have been, and their absence from **N**'s earliest layers may suggest that he achieved fame only later in his career, as discussed further later.

42 Of the 31 motets in **Tu**, 18 are also found in the later layers of **Mo** (fascicles 1, 7, and 8 and the appendix to fascicle 5), while only 7 are in **Mo**'s old corpus. On the date of **Tu**, see Catherine A. Bradley and Gaël Saint-Cricq, with Christopher Callahan, *An Introduction, Facsimile Reproduction, and Critical Edition of Turin, Biblioteca reale, varia 42* (Lucca, forthcoming).

All told, Adam's fame seems to have arrived at a relatively late stage in his activity and may even have been a somewhat retrospective project.[43] Daniel E. O'Sullivan has observed that Adam's debates with the leading Artois producer of *jeux-partis* – Jehan Bretel, who died in 1272 – are not collected in Bretel's own anthologies but are prominent in Adam's.[44] At the very least, it must have been credible that debates between Bretel and Adam could reasonably have taken place. Such debates, if indeed they really occurred, may have assumed more importance after the fact, possibly as a means of establishing Adam's lineage within the tradition of great Arras trouvères. Significantly, the reference presumed to be to Adam in Baude Fastoul's *Congé* – which pre-dates this same year, 1272 – identifies him, by means of his father, as 'the son of maistre Henri, Adan' (not in his own right as 'de la Halle' or 'li Bocus' or as 'maistre'), while the trouvère Lambert Ferri is named in full. Symes believes that Adam, whose death is announced in the fictional *Jeu du pelerin* included within his *opera omnia* in **Ha**, was genuinely already dead when this manuscript was compiled and that **Ha** was a 'memorial anthology'.[45] If so, and since Adam's father would apparently then have outlived him, a tragically early demise before the mid-1290s could have boosted Adam's fame.[46] Equally though, **Ha** – unusual in its inclusion of both monophony and polyphony – could have been, or at least begun life as, a (successful) vanity project masterminded by Adam himself.

John Haines's description of Adam, as a 'self-promoting songwriter', tallies with Adam's unusual preoccupation with self-quotation, and possibly also with an aggrandising construction of his own history and legacy.[47] I suggest in Chapter 3 that *Entre Adam/Chief bien seans/APTATUR* may be a retrospective memorialisation of Adam's musical youth, a project consonant with the prominence afforded in his oeuvre to his *jeux-partis* with Jehan Bretel, which was not matched in Bretel's own. For a composer apparently active before 1272, Adam's absence from sources dated in this decade is as striking as his presence in those from the 1290s on, when he seems already to have been dead. After 1290, Adam's own works were included in **Mo 7**; he was quoted in **Mo 7**, in *Renart le nouvel*, and in the *Dit de la panthere*;

---

43 This is suggested also by the absence of Adam's songs from what Saint-Cricq 2019, 163, characterises as the grand collection 'of "classic" trouvère song' represented by the four related chansonniers **Trouv. K**, **Trouv. N**, **Trouv. P**, and **Trouv. X**, thought to have been copied in Artois or Picardy in the 1270s or 1280s (on which see 176 n. 70).

44 O'Sullivan 2019, 164.

45 See Symes 2019, 22.

46 On the death of Adam's father, see n. 19.

47 Haines 2019, 119; Ibos-Augé 2019, 251 n. 12, notes that self-quotation is unusual in the broader song corpus, and is practised by only three other trouvères.

and his songs were added to join those of other Artesian greats in **N**.[48] Adam, therefore, apparently assumed more status as an older or even posthumous master around 1290 than he did as an active young composer in (presumably) the 1270s and 1280s. This could partly have been thanks to a deliberate re-fashioning of Adam's earlier reputation, and possibly also in reaction to his death as a relatively young man.

'Finding' Song

The compositional activities of Adam and Petrus may have overlapped, but on the whole, the stylistic, chronological, and circumstantial evidence suggests that Petrus's motets post-dated those of Adam. In the specific case of the 'Aucun' incipit, the broader semantic context of Petrus's *Aucun ont trouve* bears out the conclusion that he was quoting Adam's *Aucun se sont loe* incipit, and with the pointed addition of individual syllables to Adam's formerly melismatic semibreves.[49] 'Some have composed (*trouve*) their songs from habit', Petrus's triplum begins, 'but love, who re-emboldens my desire, gives me reason for it, so that I have to make (*faire*) a song'.[50] Petrus explicitly sets his own process of composition in opposition to 'Some' who remain unnamed, but the very word 'Aucun', together with its accompanying musical material, identifies Adam. As in the fascicle 8 triplum *Se je sui* discussed in Chapter 1, Adam's motet incipit stands in *Aucun ont trouve* as an evocation of an older manner of song-making that is explicitly contrasted with – and here actually updated in – a newer syllabic semibreve style. The positive view of love espoused in Petrus's *Aucun ont trouve* text as a whole, and in the texts of the two additional 'Aucun' tripla in this same rhythmic style in **Mo** 7 and 8, directly contradicts Adam's denunciation of love in *Aucun se sont loe*. Again in opposition to Adam, Petrus's more extravagant syllabic semibreve style is, as Maw has proposed, itself a depiction of the desire that inspires him, and it is true love that is the ultimate justification,

48 On probable quotations of Adam in *Renart le Nouvel* (dated after 1291), see Saltzstein 2019b, 354–55. On quotations of Adam in the *Dit de la panthere* – dated between 1290 and 1328 – see Huot 1987a, 193–94 and 201–02.

49 In the polyphonic quotation of Adam's rondeau refrain in his motet, the relationship between Adam's motet triplum and rondeau triplum is less exact than it could have been (compare Examples 1.1 and 1.2). This could indicate that Adam combined a quotation of Petrus's 'Aucun' incipit with a simultaneous polyphonic quotation of his own rondeau (a similar opening triple quotation to that which Adam achieves in *De ma dame/Dieus, comment/OMNES*). However, it is equally likely that Adam's 'Aucun' incipit was influenced – intentionally or subconsciously – by the motetus of *Aucuns m'ont/ANGELUS* and deviated from his own rondeau triplum as a result.

50 This translation is adapted from Maw 2018, 181.

as well as the motivation, for his unusual and somewhat strange multi-sem-ibreve declamations.[51]

Petrus's choice of the initial verb 'trouver' – literally 'to find', but here meaning 'to compose' (employed in the same sense as in the noun trouvère) – may carry an additional significance.[52] Even within the repertoire of vernacu-lar songs, which often reflect on the act of their own creation, the usual verb to describe the act of composition is 'faire' ('to make'), while 'trouver' is employed only rarely.[53] As in songs, motets in **Mo** overwhelmingly prefer the phrase 'faire un chant' or 'chanson', occasionally specifically referring to the 'making' of a 'quadruble' or 'treble'; in one instance a motetus states that it 'would like to make a little motet' ('voil faire un motet petit', in **Mo** 5, no. 82).[54] In conjunction with a quotation of Adam's 'Aucun' incipit – itself more common as the first word of a song than of a motet – the selection of the particular verb 'trouver' in the first line of *Aucun ont trouve* is therefore noteworthy. Not only does it enable a rhyme with *Aucun se sont loe* and cre-ate a lexical variety that additionally heightens the sense of contrast between Adam and Petrus's modes of composition, but it might also invoke Adam's principal identity as a trouvère songwriter. Petrus, in his motet, seems there-fore to embrace the inspiration of love to 'make' polyphony in a new way, one that responds to and departs from that of a trouvère like Adam, whose own rejection of love is invoked here as an old-fashioned style in which songs were 'found', out of habit.

51 Ibid., 181–83.
52 I have found only three additional instances in **Mo** where 'trouver' is used in the sense of 'to compose'. Two are in a construction where it is explained that love 'me fait cest chant trouver' (i.e. love made me compose this song, in the triplum of **Mo** 5, no. 115 and motetus of **Mo** 7, no. 256). The third is in the motetus of **Mo** 7, no. 292, where again love is the motivation 'de chanchon trouver', and 'trouver' falls at the end of a line, rhyming with other '-er' endings.
53 Mason 2021, 34, identifies 122 songs that use the verb 'faire', while only 26 employ 'trouver', and the expression 'commencier' (to commence) a song is more typical, used in 33 songs. 'Commencier chanson' is very uncommon in motets, but it is used by Petrus, in the motetus of **Mo** 7, no. 253. I thank Joseph W. Mason for sharing his work in advance of publication.
54 The use of the verb 'faire' in conjunction with 'chant' or 'chanson' is found, for instance, in the tripla of **Mo** fascicle 3, no. 42; fascicle 5, nos. 95, 116, and 128; fascicle 7, no. 293; and fascicle 8, nos. 316 and 324. **Mo** 3, no. 50 has 'ai fet un novel deschant', while **Mo** 2, no. 30 uses 'faire' to refer to a 'quadruble', and **Mo** 5, no. 116 (as well as 'fere chancon') refers specifically to making a 'treble'. **Mo** 5, no. 131 states that 'cest treble fis acorder a deus chans' ('this triplum has been made to accord with two voices'), an expression shared with **Mo** 5, no. 114, which explains that 'Amours . . . me fet ce treble acorder' ('love made me accord this triplum'). See the discussion of several of these **Mo** motets that reflect on their own processes of composition in Rose-Steel 2011, 50–57.

3   People and Places

Adam and an 'Entre . . .' Motet Tradition

The previous chapter established interconnections between **Mo** fascicle 7 and 8 motets with the shared opening word 'Aucun'. Another tradition surrounding a triplum text incipit, and one also associated with Adam, is evident among three motets recorded in **Mo** 7 whose tripla begin with the word 'Entre'. In contrast with the 'Aucun' incipit, to which no significance had previously been attached, interconnections between 'Entre' motets in fascicle 7 have long been recognised.[1] The three 'Entre' tripla are closely related and relatively idiosyncratic in their content, describing life 'between' certain young friends, who are explicitly named at the outset. In 1898, Henri Guy transcribed these triplum texts as part of a group from the final fascicles of **Mo** that he identified as 'student motets'.[2] Friedrich Ludwig subsequently traced connections between the friends named across these separate tripla.[3] And Mark Everist recently proposed that the communities evoked in these texts might, in fact, be confraternities.[4] This chapter re-examines this group of six motet tripla in the final fascicles of **Mo**, which share a preoccupation with people and places (see Table 3.1).[5] Four of the tripla name at least four

---

1   See Guy 1898, 79–83; Besseler 1927, 164; Ludwig 1978, 558–59; Gallo 1985 (1977), 25–27; Everist 2018, 24–28.
2   Guy 1898, 79–83. In addition to the three 'Entre' texts, Guy's corpus of 'motets des étudiants' includes the **Mo** 8 tripla *Dieus, comment pourrai laissier* and *A maistre Jehan Lardier*.
3   See the entry for *A maistre Jehan Lardier* in Ludwig 1978, 558–59.
4   Everist 2018, 24–28. Like Besseler and Gallo (see n. 1), Everist's corpus includes the **Mo** 8 motet *On parole/A Paris/FRESE NOUVELE*. He underlines references to 'compagnions' in these texts, and most notably to 'la compagnie' in the less pleasure-focused and more moralising *Dieus, comment pourrai*, which is additionally combined with a sacred motetus. Everist notes (at 27) that the names of Adam's friends (Hancart and Gautelot) might also be identifiable with those who belonged to the Confraternity of Jongleurs and Bourgeois in Arras.
5   I do not include the motetus of the **Mo** 8 unicum *L'autre jour/L'autrier, joiant et joli/ VILAIN, LIEVE SUS O* (no. 313), which has not previously been connected with the group of works discussed earlier, but which meets almost all of the content criteria for the corpus

DOI: 10.4324/9781003259282-4

Table 3.1 'Entre' and related motets

Motet (relevant text(s) highlighted in bold, in **Mo** order)	Concordances	Place	Names (variants indicated)	Reference to 'compaignons'	References to music
Entre Copin et Bourgois/ Je me cuidoie/ *BELE YSABELOS*	**Mo** 7, no. 256 **Tu**, no. 16 **Bes**, no. 30 **Ba**, no. 52	Paris	Copin Bourgois (**Mo**), Bourjois (**Ba**), Borgois (**Tu**) Hanicot (Hanikot in **Tu**) Charlot Pierron (**Mo**), Perron (**Ba**), Pieron (**Tu**)	loial compaignon	—
Entre Adam et Haniket/ Chief bien seans/ *APTATUR*	**Ha** **Mo** 7, no. 258 **Bes**, no. 28 **Ba**, no. 24 **Tu**, no. 2 **Vorau**	?Arras (inferred from local names and expressions)	Adan (Adam in **Tu**) Hanikel (**Ha** and **Tu**), Haniket (**Mo**), Henequel (**Ba**) Hancart (Hankart in **Tu** and **Vorau**) Gautelot	—	hoquetent frestel chantent tout sans livre
Entre Jehan et Philippet/ Nus hom ne puet desiervir/ *CHOSE TASSIN*	**Mo** 7, no. 294 (Supplement 1)	—	Jehan Philippet Bertaut Estievenet	—	bien chanter
Dieus, comment porrai/ O regina/ *NOBIS CONCEDAS*	**Mo** 8, no. 307	Paris	—	la vie des compaignons a Paris la compaignie	jouer chanter

(*Continued*)

Motet (relevant text(s) highlighted in bold, in **Mo** order)	Concordances	Place	Names (variants indicated)	Reference to 'compaignons'	References to music
On parole/ **A Paris**/ FRESE NOUVELE	**Mo** 8, no. 319	Paris (triplum and motetus)	–	bons compaignons (triplum) toutes guises compaignons (motetus)	chantans (triplum)
A maistre Jehan Lardier/ Pour la plus/ ALLELUYA	**Mo** 8, no. 334	Companions in Paris addressed from the 'north' ('no paiis')	Maistre Jehan Lardier Tibaut Climent le Joli Hannicote Marc d'Argent Copin Martin de Bernartpre Franque Huet le Burier Maistre Petit l'Alose Pierre l'Engles	[A. . .] toutes les autres compaignons bons	–

specific individuals, of which three adopt an 'Entre' opening, and four of them mention companions in Paris. In this chapter, for the first time, I situate the 'Entre' motets in their broader monophonic context and engage with questions of chronology and modelling. I further reflect on conceptualisations of musical community and geography within the final fascicles of **Mo**, demonstrating that these layers of the motet repertoire betray a particular interest in describing and naming groups of musical companions, at least some of whom were also composers.

The 'Entre' Opening in Motets and Songs

Adam de la Halle's *Entre Adam et Haniket/Chief bien seans/APTATUR* was not only the best known of his own motets – surviving in six different musical sources – but also the most widely transmitted example of an 'Entre' motet. *Entre Adam et Haniket*, the sixth piece in **Mo** fascicle 7, is separated here by only one intervening composition from *Entre Copin et Bourgois/ Je me cuidoie/BELE YSABELOS.*[6] The latter is the fourth motet in **Mo** fascicle 7, and it survives in three further sources (**Ba**, **Bes**, and **Tu**), all of which also preserve *Entre Adam et Haniket* (see Table 3.1).[7] While these two 'Entre' motets apparently circulated in conjunction, the third – *Entre Jehan et Philippet/Nus hom ne puet desiervir/CHOSE TASSIN* – is extant uniquely in **Mo** 7's first supplement.

The 'Entre' opening, like its 'Aucun' counterpart, is consistently confined to triplum voices in **Mo** 7, although unlike the musical 'Aucun' incipit shared between Adam and Petrus, the opening melodic gestures of the three 'Entre' tripla are not related. As in the case of 'Aucun' as a poetic opening, 'Entre' has a richer and more established tradition as an incipit for songs rather than motets, and it is a typical first word for a pastourelle.[8] 'Entre'

---

in Table 3.1. The motetus simply reports that two companions ('doi compaignon'), Terri and Simon, went out from Orléans towards Clari, exercising their dogs and singing ('tout chantant') with joyful and amorous hearts. It thus names two companions, as well as a specific location – this time south of Paris – and additionally refers to music-making. However, the motetus is a brief and formally much more conventional text than the tripla in Table 3.1. In common with many earlier motets in the pastourelle idiom, it opens with the expression 'L'autrier' and closes with a refrain.

6 *Entre Adam et Haniket* and *Entre Copin et Bourgois* are compared in Huot 1997, 32–36.
7 *Entre Copin et Bourgois* comes first only in **Mo** 7, while Adam's motet precedes it in **Ba**, **Bes**, and **Tu** (see Table 3.1 for details). As in **Mo** 7, the two motets are close in **Bes**, separated only by a single (different) intervening motet (and in the reverse order). In **Tu**, Adam's motet is the second in the collection, while *Entre Copin* is the sixteenth. In **Ba**, the position of compositions follows the alphabetical ordering of this source by motetus incipit (with the result that *Entre Adam* comes first).
8 'Entre', although more so than 'Aucun', was not widespread as a refrain opening. It begins just two refrains in van den Boogaard's catalogue: *'Entre glai et fueille et flour et violette'*

usually sets up an opposition between two places – specific towns (as in *Entre Arras et Douai*, RS 75) or generic locales (in *Entre lo bois et la plaine*, RS 141) – or two characters, which can equally be named (as in *Entre Godefroi et Robin*, RS 1377) or designated by type (in *Entre moi et mon ami*, RS 1029).[9] Beyond their incipits, many of these pastourelle texts go on to refer to further locations and/or names, usually those of stock pastourelle characters such as Emmelot or Dorenlot. 'Entre' was also used to oppose named locations in several Occitan songs, and it seems to have assumed the status of the classic pastourelle opening in the later fourteenth-century French tradition for this genre: six of the eight pastourelle texts attributed to Jean Froissart begin with 'Entre', invariably opposing to two named locations.[10]

In song texts, then, there is a long and widespread practice in which 'Entre' initiates the naming of specific places and characters. By contrast, 'Entre' features as an incipit for only five motets: beyond the three tripla in **Mo** 7, just two unique two-voice motets – *Entre Robin et Marot/ET ILLUMINARE*, in **W2**, and *Antre Soixons et Paris*, a motetus text in **Douce 308** – employ this opening word.[11] It seems that the 'Entre' tripla in **Mo** capitalise on the conventional associations of this widespread song opening, otherwise employed to a limited degree in motets. The three **Mo** 7 tripla offer a new, real-life, urban, and notably personalised twist on their pastourelle incipit, using it to launch the description of a community of named personalities – twice explicitly identified as musicians – and in all cases revealed to be young men.

Adam as Instigator of the 'Entre' Tripla?

It may have been Adam who inspired a late thirteenth-century adoption of 'Entre' as the opening word of a motet triplum, like he did for 'Aucun,' as

---

(vdB 686) and '*Entre mes bras*' (vdB 687). The song corpus for 'Entre' openings could be enlarged by the inclusion of complete opening phrases in which 'Entre' features, though not as the initial word (as in *L'autrier par la matinee entre un bois et un vergier*, RS 529).

9 'Entre' is also used in more abstract contexts for opposing motivations or characteristics, as, for example, in *Entre raison et amour* (RS 740) or *Entre raison et jolive pensee* (RS 543).

10 Four Occitan songs with 'Entre' incipits are listed in in Paden 1987, vol. 2, 690. Froissart's pastourelle texts are edited in Bartsch 1870, 321–37.

11 Gennrich 1957, nos. 104 and 1094 respectively. The 'Entre' locution is used, not as an opening, but at the end of the motet *D'une amour sui sospris/ANGELUS*, uniquely recorded in **Mo** (fascicle 6, no. 198). The motet concludes 'thus, between Arras and Douai I will sing this song' ('si k'entre Arras et Douay/ceste chancon chanterai'). Saint-Cricq 2017, xxxii, notes that this turn of phrase is reminiscent of 'certain verses from monophonic entries in the poetry competitions, or "tournois," held in Arras'. Moreover, the connection between monophonic and polyphonic spheres is strengthened here, since the motet names the same two cities as the pastourelle *Entre Arras et Douai*, RS 75.

suggested in Chapter 2.[12] Arras is named as one of the places 'between' which 'Entre' pastourelles situate themselves, and as a trouvère native to this town, Adam was probably aware of this local convention.[13] Of all the 'Entre' motets in **Mo** 7, Adam's – as for the 'Aucun' motets – is stylistically the most conservative. The tripla *Entre Copin et Bourgois* and *Entre Jehan et Philippet* are dominated throughout by texted semibreves. In *Entre Copin et Bourgois* these invariably are semibreve pairs, but *Entre Jehan et Philippet* frequently also divides the breve into three syllabic semibreves and, on two occasions, into four. In addition, both of these motets are built not on quotations from plainchant but rather on secular tenor melodies, a late thirteenth-century technique discussed further in Chapter 5. By contrast, and as previously emphasised, *Entre Adam et Haniket* is rather old-fashioned in the context of vernacular motets in fascicle 7. Had Adam's motet been copied among the three-voice vernacular motets in fascicle 5 of **Mo**'s old corpus, it would not have been the most stylistically innovative motet in this collection. The declamation of motetus and triplum voices is principally in longs and breves; the breve is never divided into as many as three syllabic semibreves; and pairs of texted semibreves feature in the triplum only twice.[14] Adam's motet has a plainchant foundation and it uses the third rhythmic mode in its upper voices, a feature shared with all three of the motets on the same APTATUR melisma in **Mo**'s old corpus, but with none other of the motets on this tenor in fascicles 7 or 8.[15]

12 Previous discussions of the 'Entre' opening have not engaged with questions of chronology. In Guy's initial discussion of his five 'student' motets, he presumed that this was originally a Parisian tradition, to which Adam's motet must respond. Noting the especially close connection between *Entre Adam et Haniket* and *Entre Jehan et Philippet* demonstrated later, Guy 1898, 83, stated that the latter motet must have been the Parisian point of departure for Adam's text.

13 On the possibility of an Arras connection for the 'Entre' opening, see n. 11. In general, the places named in 'Entre' openings are not south of Paris.

14 In the copy of *Entre Adam et Haniket* in **Ba** there is an error in the triplum in both places where the semibreve pairs appear (on fol. 13v). For the first pair of semibreves, the word 'que' was initially omitted and later inserted above the text line. For the second, the two semibreves were copied, not with the correct diamond shape, but rather as square breves (here left uncorrected). Potentially, therefore, the two isolated instances of semibreve pairs in this triplum were later, 'updated', modifications to this motet, whose implementation posed challenges for the **Ba** scribe.

15 The upper voices of *Psallat chorus/Eximie pater/APTATUR* (**Mo** 4, no. 60) and *He Marotele/En la praierie/APTATUR* (**Mo** 5, no. 75, and the contrafactum of this motet as **Mo** 5, no. 146 with the texts *He mere Diu/La virge Marie/APTATUR*) are squarely in mode 3. *Joliement/Quant voi/Je sui joliete/APTATUR* (**Mo** 2, no. 34) mixes passages of declamation in mode 3, mode 2 (especially prevalent in motetus and triplum voices), and mode 5. I have previously proposed that Adam instigated the APTATUR tenor melisma; see Bradley 2019, 462–65. However, despite the fact that Adam's APTATUR motet is closer

Was *Entre Adam et Haniket* an early work by Adam or rather a conservative one, by the comparative standards of his other two motets in **Mo** 7 and by those of the French-texted motets in that fascicle more generally? The text of this motet triplum could hold a clue: Adam, who heads the list of four named companions, is referred to at the motet's close as one of 'these four infants' or 'youths' ('cil quatre enfant'). Adam may genuinely have been young when he created this motet, which – though by then a little dated – was later included along with his other compositions in **Mo** 7. But in that case, one might have expected to find *Entre Adam et Haniket* already within **Mo**'s old corpus. Alternatively, Adam could have reverted to the style prevalent in his youth, retrospectively to depict – in the present tense – its joyful music-making and drunken jokes. This style is not radically archaic in the context of **Mo** 7, still less in the broader stylistic context of Adam's oeuvre as represented by the two of his motets in **Ha** that are not included in **Mo**. But the old-fashioned, modal idiom of *Entre Adam et Haniket* is more noticeable in the context of **Tu**, where – unlike in **Mo** 7 – it was the sole representative of Adam's work.

Adam's triplum states that he and his friends 'sing everything without books, old and new' ('si chantent tout sans livre/vies et nouvel'), and this reveals a historical perspective with regard to song that may be interpretatively significant. Perhaps Adam's self-referential motet was intended and/ or later perceived as a stylistic evocation of the musical past. As discussed in Chapter 1, this is how a quotation of *Chief bien seans* is explicitly framed in fascicle 8, where Adam's slow-moving and melismatic motetus incipit stands out at the conclusion of the more rapidly declaimed and entirely syllabic **Mo** 8 triplum *Se je sui*, whose text declares its own song to be more expressive than Adam's. In any case, the fame of *Entre Adam et Haniket* would plausibly have increased either because it circulated for a comparatively long time while Adam was still living, or because it appealed as a retrospective and nostalgic evocation of his musical youth.

Naming Motets

The motet *Entre Copin et Bourgois*, surviving exclusively in sources also containing *Entre Adam et Haniket*, likewise depicts the activities of young friends, but here in a more up-to-date musical idiom. *Entre Copin et Bourgois*

---

stylistically to those in the old corpus than to others in **Mo** 7 and 8, these old-corpus motets are more archaic in the rhythmic arrangement of their APTATUR tenors than Adam's. Furthermore, if Adam's motets became known sometime between the copying of **Mo**'s old corpus and fascicle 7 – as proposed in Chapter 2 – it is unlikely that Adam himself was responsible for the introduction of the APTATUR tenor.

opens by naming five 'loyal companions' ('loial compaignon') – Copin, Bourgois, Hanicot, Charlot, and Pierron – who live in Paris. However, the main body of the triplum text continues with a description of the love of one of them (whose identity is kept secret) for a fair Ysabelot, also the love object of the motet's song tenor. Since this love has caused the anonymous lover to 'miss many a lesson' ('perdre mainte lecon'), these Parisian friends must – as Guy and Huot observed – be students.[16]

Entre Copin et Bourgois is clearly of the same poetic type as *Entre Adam et Haniket* and the additional 'Entre' motet in the first supplement to fascicle 7, *Entre Jehan et Philippet*. Yet *Entre Adam et Haniket* and *Entre Jehan et Philippet* are slightly different in emphasis, focused throughout on the revelries of friends as a group, rather than the love story of one of them. Moreover, these two tripla are so closely related that one must be directly modelled on the other (see Table 3.2).[17] Both motets follow almost exactly the same narrative outline, often with shared vocabulary and the same conjunctions to introduce each new section of the text (highlighted in bold in Table 3.2).[18] The motets each concern a different community of four named friends, who experience great joy when they sing together, but only after they have been drinking. Then follows an account of how the fourth-named friend (Gautelot or Estievenet) loves to play the fool. Only after these descriptions do the two texts diverge slightly in their content (highlighted by italics in Table 3.2): Adam's motet discusses how the so-called windmill ('moulin') is danced by all four friends, while *Entre Jehan et Philippet* focuses instead on just the third-named friend (Biertaus), who pretends to be out of his senses. Closing with similar concluding couplets, both motets return to the theme of the great joy of the 'four youths' ('quatre enfant/enfans').

While *Entre Copin et Bourgois* is a song about five Parisian students of good reputation, not explicitly identified as musicians, just four musical and

---

16 See Guy 1898, 79–83; Huot 1997, 35.

17 Guy 1898, 83, first noted this correspondence, which has not subsequently been examined in detail, perceiving that *Entre Adam et Haniket* contained 'almost identical phrases' ('des phrases presque identiques') to *Entre Jehan et Philippet* and must have stemmed from a 'common source' ('source commune'). Guy assumed that this was a Parisian tradition of 'student motets' to which Adam responded. More recently, Ferreira 1998, 96, in his discussion of temporal construction in **Mo** motets, noted the initial correspondence of characters' activities in *Entre Adam et Haniket* and *Entre Jehan et Philippet*, proposing that the texts were from the 'same poetic family' ('la même famille poétique').

18 In two instances the motets interchange vocabulary: *Entre Adam et Haniket* refers to 'esbanoi' at the opening and 'deduisant' at its close, while the respective positions of these synonyms are reversed in *Entre Jehan et Philippet*. Compare the second and penultimate sections of the text in Table 3.2.

Table 3.2 Texts of *Entre Adan et Haniket* (**Mo** 7, fols. 280v–282r) and *Entre Jehan et Philippet* (**Mo** 7, fols. 336v–338r)

Shared text in bold; divergence indicated by italics.

Entre Adan et Haniket	Entre Jehan et Philippet
Entre Adan et Haniket	**Entre** Jehan et Philippet
Hancart et Gautelot	Bertuat et Estievenet
a grant esbanoi, qui ot	**en grant** deduit sunt menu et souvent
lor revel	
quant il hoquetent	**quant il** sunt asamble,
plus tost clapetent	de bien chanter ne se faignent noient
que frestel	
li damoisel	
mais qu'il aient avant baisie	**mais** qu'il aient avant touchiet
Saint Tortuel	du boin vin cler et gent
et si chantent tout sans livre	
vies et nouvel	
Gautelos fait l'ivre	et quant **Estievenet fait** le sot,
si proprement et si bel,	il le fait **si proprement**
qu'il samble a son musel	car qui ne l'aroit
qu'il doie traire a sa fin.	onques vu, il cuideroit,
	qu'il le fust proprement.
Et quant il font le moulin	Lors saut *Biertaus*, ki fait le hors du sens
ensamble tout quatre	
et au plastre batre	
en hoquetant	
sont **si** deduisant,	**si** a grant esbaniement
si gay, **si** joiant	
et **si** riant	
cil **quatre enfant**	de **quatre enfans**
que nule **gent** tant.	qui ne font pas a refuser entre la **gent**.

slightly wilder-living young friends in an unspecified location are the protagonists of *Entre Adam et Haniket* and *Entre Jehan et Philippet*. Although no place is named, the Artesian flavour of Adam's motet has been noted, including his local euphemism ('kissing Saint Tortuel') for having a drink, the presence of what seem to be family names from Arras (Hancart and Gautelot), and possibly also the APTATUR tenor drawn from the Office of the northern French saint Winnoc of Bergues.[19] Potentially, the tenor of

19 See Rokseth 1935–39, vol. 4, 288, for a discussion of local expressions in this text. On the names Hancart and Gautelot as native to Arras, see Everist 2018, 27. On the origins of the APTATUR tenor, see Goudesenne 2000. See also Bradley 2019, 462–65.

Entre Jehan et Philippet also hints at a locale, this time in Paris. Three (different) tenor melodies in **Mo** 7 are labelled CHOSE TASSIN, a 'thing' associated with someone called Tassin. Yvonne Rokseth identified Tassin as one of King Philippe le Bel's minstrels, listed in royal accounts for 1288.[20] She suggested, convincingly, that he was probably also the instrumentalist Tassinus, mentioned in the *Ars musice* of Johannes de Grocheio (which, on the basis of its content, must post-date Franco's treatise) as a creator of 'difficult pieces' in the estampie genre.[21]

One cannot infer too much about the date of *Entre Jehan et Philippet* from that of the documentary evidence which happens to survive for the musician who gave his name to its tenor. Nevertheless, it is plausible that Tassin's reputation was at or near its height when he held a desirable position at the royal court in the late 1280s and that the melodies explicitly attributed to him were also adopted as motet tenors around this time.[22] This, in turn, would be in sympathy with the 1290s dating of **Mo** 7, where Tassin's three tenors exclusively appear. The internal evidence of **Mo** 7 itself supports the conclusion that *Entre Jehan et Philippet*, a unicum motet added in the fascicle's first supplement and which exceeds the triple division of the breve permitted by Lambertus and Franco, was explicitly responding to Adam's much more widely transmitted triplum already recorded in the fascicle's main body and in the more conservative idiom of the third rhythmic mode.

The modelling of *Entre Jehan et Philippet* on *Entre Adam et Haniket* seems to confirm that the latter motet was not only the best-known example of the 'Entre' opening but also that Adam was its instigator in this group of interconnected motets. Since Adam's *Entre Adam et Haniket* names the composer as the first of the protagonists, it is possible that the Parisian student Copin was the creator of *Entre Copin et Bourgois*, and that Jehan composed *Entre Jehan et Philippet*, whose CHOSE TASSIN tenor suggests a Parisian location. The direct connection between *Entre Adam et Haniket* and *Entre Jehan et Philippet* makes Jehan's status as a motet composer especially plausible. This may

---

20 Rokseth 1935–39, vol. 4, 290.
21 For the relevant passage of Grocheio's treatise, see the edition and translation by Mews et al. 2011, 74–75. Despite the 1288 date for Tassinus, these authors date Grocheio's treatise in the 1270s (at 9), largely on the basis of cultural context. They place Franco's *Ars cantus* in the 1260s on the dubious grounds that all of Franco's musical examples date from before the mid-thirteenth century. On the evidence for the accepted c.1280 date for Franco's treatise, see Chapter 2.
22 In the incomplete 1292 census of Paris – on which see n. 29 – there are listed four Tassins. In relation to the other tenor of this type in **Mo** 7, CHOSE LOYSET, presumably also naming an instrumentalist, there is one Loyset. He is the son of Phelippe le pévrier (literally pepper seller) and has some money of his own, suggesting that he is not too young to be an established musician before 1290. The census records a single de la Halle (Bertaut) and the closest approximation to Petrus's surname is de la Croiz, for which there are eight instances but none with the name Pierre.

be borne out by an additional and related motet, uniquely recorded in **Mo** 8, whose triplum does not use the 'Entre' incipit, but rather opens by addressing a list of named characters of which the first is a 'Maistre Jehan'.

The triplum of *A maistre Jehan Lardier/Pour la plus/ALLELUYA* is directed to a roll of eleven individuals, of which Copin and Hanicot/Hannicote (and possibly also Pierron as Pierre l'Engles) match the Parisian friends in *Entre Copin et Bourgois* (see the complete list of names in Table 3.1).[23] In common with *Entre Copin et Bourgois*, musical activities are not explicitly mentioned for the eleven friends and 'all the other good companions' ('toutes les autres compaignons bons') greeted in *A maistre Jehan Lardier*, but their location in Paris is confirmed and at least maistre Jehan Lardier and a 'maistre Petit l'Alose' would appear to have received a university education, conferring on them the title of Master.[24] Unlike all of the 'Entre' motets, *A maistre Jehan Lardier* is in the first-person voice, and of someone who regrets that, for the sake of love, he is in the north of the country.[25] He asks after his friends and a merry life in Paris, of which he clearly once had firsthand experience: '[Amours] me tient en no paiis, et que fait ore Paris?'[26]

Did the fascicle 8 triplum *A maistre Jehan Lardier* – which Christopher Page characterises as a parody of an official letter – address the Jehan who was himself the composer of the *Entre Jehan et Philippet* motet in the first supplement to fascicle 7, a composition which, in turn, was modelled directly on Adam's *Entre Adam et Haniket*, preserved in fascicle 7's main body?[27] The use of the title 'maistre' is applied to both Adam and Petrus as

---

23 This was first noted in the discussion of *A maistre Jehan Lardier* in Ludwig 1978, 558–59.

24 On the title 'maistre' and its association with a university education (if not strictly with the teaching licence that the appellation officially carried), see Saltzstein 2012, 152. The translation of 'Jehan Lardier' as 'John the butcher' in Stakel and Relihan 1985, 115, seems unlikely. It is probable that Lardier is simply a family name or a byname, especially since any definite article is lacking in the motet. In the catalogue of bynames for medieval France in Uckelman 2014, Lardier is included as a byname found in several late thirteenth- and early fourteenth-century Picard sources, although here (unlike in the motet) it is prefaced by a definite article, making the indication of a profession more likely.

25 It is not clear why Everist 2018, 24, considers 'no paiis' to be north of Lille.

26 Rokseth 1935–39, vol. 4, 300, aligned this **Mo** 8 motet with Adam's style (specifically in *Aucun se sont loe/A Dieu commant/SUPER TE*). The *A maistre Jehan Lardier* triplum uses mainly pairs of texted semibreves, with only one trio: possibly this motet was either a conservative or archaic composition or a genuinely old work that was included in fascicle 8 because of its connections to the fascicle 7 motets. On the fact that the majority of characters named in *A maistre Jehan* cannot be identified within the admittedly incomplete Parisian census of 1292 see n. 29.

27 See Page 1993, 98. That *A maistre Jehan Lardier* does not name any of the other companions mentioned in *Entre Jehan et Philippet* could be an argument against identifying the Jehan of *Entre Jehan et Philippet* with Jehan Lardier. *A maistre Jehan* does not name Adam

well, and this would put Jehan Lardier – who takes pride of place among the eleven characters addressed in the **Mo** 8 triplum – in a similar category, that of a skilled and educated composer.[28] Chronologically, the various layers of **Mo** fit with the narratives of the cast of characters: the fascicle 8 motet *A maistre Jehan Lardier* refers back to several of the Parisian student friends in fascicle 7's *Entre Copin et Bourgois* – and possibly also to the (composer?) Jehan of *Entre Jehan et Philippet* – in order to reminisce wistfully about the same kinds of Parisian activities previously described, in **Mo**'s preceding 'Entre' motets, in the present tense.[29]

Paris and the 'North'

The anonymous triplum singer or composer in *A maistre Jehan Lardier* sends south nostalgic greetings in song to former Parisian friends. While this poetic text cannot be taken too literally, neither could its scenario have been wholly unrelatable. Indeed, the situation described in *A maistre Jehan Lardier* chimes with what has been imagined both for Adam and for Petrus, both northern composers who probably studied in Paris and then went back

---

or any of his friends either, perhaps suggesting that Adam was not, or no longer, in Paris, and/or that he belonged to a different (possibly earlier) generation.

28 On Adam's status as 'maistre', a title that he receives in the eulogic *Jeu du pelerin*, but not in his own songs or *jeux-partis*, see Corbellari 2019, 233–38. Petrus's association with this title is more certain: he appears as 'magister' in the 1298 royal treasury accounts (see Johnson 1991, 474–75) and in the Amiens census of 1301–2 as 'maistres', one of only two in this large household to carry this title (see Johnson 1991, 467; see also Garnier 1859, 204–06). Petrus was not, however, described as 'magister' by Jacobus – who himself had this status – but rather as a 'worthy singer' ('valens cantor'). By contrast, Jacobus frequently refers to 'Magister Franco'. See Bent 2015, 22–24.

29 Most of the names listed in *A maistre Jehan Lardier* are absent from the Parisian census of 1292; see Géraud 1837; Uckelman 2013. Crucially, though, the census is incomplete, since it omits much of the left bank. Of the 11 people named in this motet, five are given additional bynames or surnames that could render them identifiable. The 1292 census has entries for two of these: there is a single 'd'Argent' and five 'Marc-d'Argent's, and multiple variants and instances of the identifier 'l'Englés' (English). There are, however, no entries that could reasonably be identified with 'Lardier', 'de Bernartpre', 'le Burier', or 'l'Alose'. Of course, these people may simply have lived in parts of Paris not included in the census. Yet if the majority of addressees in *A maistre Jehan* were not, indeed, in the city in 1292 this is open to several interpretations. Perhaps they arrived in Paris after 1292, a *terminus post quem* for *A maistre Jehan*. Alternatively, despite the fact that that this motet first appears uniquely in fascicle 8, the piece could predate 1292 (see n. 26). The community addressed in *A maistre Jehan* would have been fairly transient if indeed most of its members had either already left or not yet arrived in Paris by 1292. Potentially, then, the triplum's anonymous composer named friends who might – as he had – have spent only a short time in Paris, possibly as students.

to their home towns.[30] It seems that Adam later married and settled in Arras, while Petrus was back in his native Amiens in the early fourteenth century.[31] I do not propose that the unidentified narrator of *A maistre Jehan Lardier* was either Adam or Petrus. Rather, I suggest that their personal and professional trajectories were possibly quite typical, and underline the degree of travel and exchange between northern French-speaking lands and Paris.

Northern composers are afforded considerable status in **Mo** 7 and 8, collections probably compiled in Paris. Fascicle 7 begins with works by Petrus, contains multiple quotations of Adam, as well as – as discussed in Chapter 4 – a motetus voice thought to be a song by the older Amiens trouvère Richard de Fournival and a KYRIE tenor whose trope text was not common as far south as Paris. Rokseth, while cautioning that the orthography of a motet text is not a direct indication of its provenance, nonetheless notes that Petrus's first two motets in fascicle 7 are in quite pronounced Picard dialect and that strong Picard taints are especially evident also among motets in the first supplement to fascicle 7.[32] In addition, the song tenor of two unica in fascicle 8 features the text 'Defors Compeigne', naming a city in the south of Picardy, between Paris and Amiens on the river Oise.[33]

The evident activity of northern composers both in their home towns and in Paris encourages further reconsideration of the fading presumption, not only that the genre of the motet itself is quintessentially Parisian, but also

30 It is presumed that both Adam and Petrus studied in Paris, since they received the title 'maistre' (see n. 28). In the thirteenth century, Paris was the closest French university to either Arras or Amiens. For Adam, there is additional contextual evidence: his fictional *Jeu d'Adam* states that he wishes to resume his studies in Paris, and (as noted in Saltzstein 2012, 150) Jehan Bretel refers to Adam as 'well lettered' ('bien letres'). If, however, *Entre Adam et Haniket* pertains to drinking and singing in student days, then this seems to have been not in Paris but Arras (or at least with Arras friends). This may be further confirmation that *Entre Adam et Haniket* was a retrospective and somewhat fictionalised reimagining of Adam's youth.

31 This is inferred principally from Adam's dramatic works, which are set in Arras, and from his mention, in the *Jeu d'Adam*, of a wife in Arras ('Maroie') as well as his father (a 'Maistre Henri de la Halle', whose real-life identity seems to be confirmed by Fastoul's *Congé*, discussed in Chapter 2). For Petrus, the two principal pieces of documentary evidence outlined in Chapter 2 and in n. 28 confirm his Amiens origins as well as his presence there in the early fourteenth century.

32 On the danger of equating Picard dialect with a motet's origin see Rokseth 1935–39, vol. 4, 10. **Tu**, with its Walloon orthography, is instructive, since many of its motets have concordances elsewhere in which there is no trace of Walloon influence, and these compositions are not considered to come from Liège on the grounds of their appearance in **Tu**. See Rokseth 1935–39, vol. 4, 79, on the pronounced Picard dialect of Petrus's motets and at 247 on the prevalence of Picard texts in the first supplement to fascicle 7.

33 The tenor of **Mo** 8, no. 321 opens with the text 'Defors Compeigne', part of the same song that beings with the refrain '*D'un joli dart*' in the tenor of **Mo** 8, no. 309.

that motets about Paris are necessarily by native composers who live there.[34] In addition to *Entre Copin et Bourgois* and *A maistre Jehan Lardier*, two further motets in **Mo**'s final fascicles – *Dieus, comment porrai laissier/O regina/NOBIS CONCEDAS* and *On parole/A Paris/FRESE NOUVELE*, both unica in fascicle 8 – specifically mention Paris, and they also describe life among Parisian companions. Both have been connected with the 'Entre' motets and *A maistre Jehan Lardier* for this reason (even though neither actually names any companions), serving in turn to confirm Paris as the focus of this type of motet.[35] The very fascination of *Dieus, comment* and *On parole* with this city might, however, indicate that these tripla were – like *A maistre Jehan Lardier* – born out of nostalgia and separation from a place which the composers knew well and probably as students, but where they did or could not spend their entire lives.

A certain non-native Parisian romanticism might be said to pervade *Dieus, comment*, which opens by asking: 'God, how can I leave the life of the companions in Paris?' ('Dieus, comment porrai laissier la vie des compaignons a Paris?').[36] The answer, of course, is that this would be impossible because of the many good friends, as well as the laughter and joyful playing and singing that would have to be abandoned. Nevertheless, the framing of the text with the threat of departure – apparently a reality for Adam, Petrus, and the composer of *A maistre Jehan Lardier* – might be more than a mere rhetorical pose. Similarly, *On parole/A Paris/FRESE NOUVELE* is based on an imitation of a Parisian street cry, and its accompanying texts are lavish in their praise for the city to the point of idealism. The triplum, which opens by disparaging rural labour before extolling the virtues of Parisian wine, women, and song, was the product of a composer who was intimately acquainted with Paris, and whose quotation of its street cries was ostentatious proof of this. Yet the dismissal of rural life suggests that this may equally have been something experienced at first-hand by the motet's creator, who thus neither hailed from Paris nor remained there.

---

34 Saltzstein 2013; Saint-Cricq 2017 have recently challenged Paris-centred narratives of polyphony, emphasising the importance of motet composition in Arras, in relation to Adam and the Chansonnier de Noailles respectively.

35 See Everist 2018, 25–26. See also Guy 1898, 83, and the discussion in n. 17.

36 Two further motets in **Mo** 7 and 8 share this opening rhetorical question: the motetus of Adam's *De ma dame vient/Dieus, comment porroie/OMNES* in fascicle 7 (no. 279), and the triplum of the fascicle 8 unicum (no. 314) *Dieus, comment puet li cuers durer/Vo vair oel m'ont espris/TENOR*.

Community, Identity, and Authorship

In addition to their preoccupation with people and places, the six motets discussed here reveal their interest in acts of communal music-making (see Table 3.1). In just two of these tripla – *Entre Copin et Bourgois* and *A maistre Jehan Lardier* – it is not stipulated that the named companions are necessarily musicians, although the fact that their companionship is described within a song may be indication enough that they were. *On parole*, however, makes reference to singing, among other pleasures, while *Dieus, comment* mentions both 'playing' ('jouer') and singing. *Entre Jehan et Philippet* notes that its four friends sing 'well' ('bien'), but it is Adam's *Entre Adam et Haniket* that contains by far the most explicit references to music: to singing and playing of a kind of flute ('frestel'), to the performance of hockets (though which are not depicted musically here), as well as the mention of songs old and new, sung entirely without books. Adam, known to be the composer of this motet, is its first-named musician, but he is otherwise undistinguished from his three friends and, like them, referred to in the third person. This is a reminder that meanings, contexts, and identities in such motets were not necessarily made explicit. Presumably, they did not need to be, especially if the communities described in these songs were also the communities who were composing and singing them.

Such emphasis on people and places, and indeed attributions, is by no means new or exclusive to motets in **Mo** fascicles 7 and 8. Several earlier thirteenth-century compositions, many preserved in **Mo**'s old corpus itself, contain regional or personal references. One famous example of the former is the motet *Mout sont/A la cheminee/PROPTER VERITATEM*, whose Latin tenor receives a vernacular text beginning with an allusion to its original chant text, *Par verité*. The version of this motet tenor in **W2** exerts the superiority of Rhine wines over those from France, while in **Mo** fascicle 2 (no. 25), the tenor text praises the qualities of French wines while deriding those from Auxerre.[37] Another motet uniquely preserved in fascicle 5 of **Mo**, *Quant se depart/Onques ne soi amer/DOCEBIT* (no. 131) has a first-person triplum which asserts that, despite the claims of liars ('mesdisans'), 'I first made this triplum to accord with two songs' (i.e the motetus and tenor) and 'I brought it from my country in the region of Tournai'.[38]

---

37 For further discussion of these motet texts, see Wolinski 2008, 13–14. For a list and discussion of places named in **Mo** motets, see also Rokseth 1935–39, vol. 4, 30–31.

38 'C'est treble fis acorder a ii chans que primes fis . . . que je les aporter de mon pais. Ce est drois de tornoi.' I concur with Rokseth 1935–39, vol. 4, 30; Rose-Steel 2011, 54, that Tournai is the location indicated in the text, rather than Tours (as rendered in the translation in Stakel and Relihan 1985, 51).

The triplum of a further fascicle 5 motet, *De jolif cuer/Je me quidai/ET GAUDEBIT* (no. 116), opens with the statement that, because a happy heart is needed to make a pleasant triplum, its suffering first-person poet is taking a 'treble' – presumably a triplum melody – by 'seignor Gilon Ferrant'.[39]

Yet occasional examples among the motets of **Mo**'s old corpus of local colour, personal reflections on the making of a polyphonic composition, or even the exceptional attribution of a particular voice part to a named composer are subtly different in nature from the community-focused motets of fascicles 7 and 8. First-person contemplations of song-making and its motivations are a common theme of trouvère songs, and, as discussed in Chapter 4, are notably characteristic too of many of the motet texts in fascicles 7 and 8 more generally, including Petrus's triplum *Aucun ont trouve*. What is substantively different about the 'Entre' motets and *A maistre Jehan Lardier*, in particular, is their preoccupation with naming, and with describing or addressing a group of (musician) companions. In this respect, the **Mo** 7 and 8 motets, though much less elevated and intellectual in tone, seem closer conceptually to a later tradition, beginning in the fourteenth century, of so-called musician motets – whose triplum texts are principally roll calls of names, praising companies of contemporary musicians – than to earlier compositions in the same manuscript. Although different in register, this later group of five musician motets shares several characteristics with the **Mo** pieces. As Margaret Bent shows, these fourteenth-century musician motets enact various cross-references, exchanges, and allusions, and three of them contain unambiguous in-text identifications of their composers.[40] There is some overlap of the names listed in their tripla, and the tradition apparently stemmed from and responded to a single work – *Apollinis eclipsatur*, whose text reveals its author, B. de Cluny – which was very widely transmitted, while the majority of its successors survive only as unica.

Thirteenth-century singers surely knew that Adam was the composer of *Entre Adam et Haniket*, and they must have been similarly familiar with the composers of the other 'Entre' motets, whose lists of names may, or

---

39 In the **Mo** copy of the motet, Gilon Ferrant's name includes the intrusion 'petara' (on fol. 158v). This was later struck out (and is absent from the concordance for this motet in **W2**, fol. 200v) but suggests some confusion about Gilon's identity. On this motet, its two related neighbouring pieces in **Mo** 5, and the broader context of **Mo** old-corpus motets that reflect on their processes of composition, see Rose-Steel 2011, 50–57. See Chapter 2 for discussion of the terminology in these **Mo** motets, with reference to the voice parts named and the verbs employed to describe making/composing.

40 I thank Margaret Bent for her discussion of these texts and for access to her work in advance of publication. See 'Part IV: *Musicorum collegium*: The Musician Motets', in *The Motet in the Late Middle Ages* (New York and Oxford, forthcoming 2022). See also Gómez 1985, esp. 13–15, on the **Mo** motets.

may not, have included their creators in ways that were of perceptible significance to contemporary performers and listeners. This notwithstanding, the actual narrative of *Entre Adam et Haniket* is not, as emphasised earlier, itself concerned with Adam's status as its creator or his creative practices and motivations in making the motet. Rather, the triplum recounts Adam's activities as one actor within a broader musical community who drank and then sang from memory. Such motets, about and for groups of singers, may well have been sung within the informal musical environments that they described, resulting in a kind of self-reflective depiction in song of the circumstances acted out by the singing of the song itself. Yet the fact that all three of the 'Entre' motets reflect so self-consciously on youth may suggest that – like *A maistre Jehan Lardier*, which explicitly recalls better days in faraway Paris – nostalgia was the mood of these motets from the start. In such circumstances, polyphonic music-making acted as a kind of reconstructionism or escapism, a means of conjuring companions scattered by time or geography. Ultimately, and in contrast to much more self-consciously intellectual fourteenth-century musicians' motets, these compositions in **Mo** 7 and 8 serve as unpretentious and arguably quite realistic memorialisations for posterity of the informal activities of their musical communities.

4 Petrus in the Montpellier Codex

The preceding chapters have demonstrated various quotational exchanges and cross-references across the final two fascicles of **Mo**, and fascicle 7 in particular. Chapters 1 and 2 examined quotations of Adam de la Halle by Adam himself, anonymous motet composers, and Petrus de Cruce, while Chapter 3 discussed motets that were part of an interlinked practice of naming communities of musicians. This chapter turns to Petrus de Cruce, whose status as a composer figure in **Mo** 7 is at once more obvious and more ambiguous than Adam's. Pieces by and quoting Adam are dispersed across fascicle 7, but the two motets that carry definite attributions to Petrus occupy pride of place at the opening of the collection. What might constitute 'Petronian' techniques of rhythm and notation and/or a 'Petronian' style of text declamation and stratification of voices within the repertoire more generally is less clear-cut. And whether or not of all the pieces that can be identified with certain of these characteristics in **Mo**'s final fascicles and beyond should be attributed to Petrus himself remains moot. This chapter reflects on questions of Petrus's authorship and individuality, reconsidering existing definitions of a 'Petronian' corpus and revealing new connections between motets across established 'Petronian' and 'Franconian' divides.

Petrus and the Evidence of Jacobus

Evidence about Petrus's compositions and techniques comes chiefly from the fourteenth-century theorist Jacobus, who – in book 7 of his *Speculum musicae* – states that it was a certain 'worthy singer' ('valens cantor'), Petrus de Cruce, who 'began' ('incepit') the practice of notating more than three semibreves within a perfect breve.[1] This practice is significant because although, as Jacobus tells us, Petrus 'followed the art of Franco' ('et artem

---

1 See the edition and translation of this passage in Bent 2015, 22–24.

DOI: 10.4324/9781003259282-5

Franconis secutus est'), Petrus's use of between four and seven semibreves within the space of a perfect breve unit surpassed Franco's maximum number of three. The term 'Petronian', therefore, has long been applied to late thirteenth-century motets that exceed Franco's triple division of the breve and to their notation of these semibreves as individual diamond-shaped notes grouped into breve units by dots or strokes. This term has usefully been problematised by Margaret Bent, who questions the conventional rhythmic interpretation of so-called Petronian semibreves established by Willi Apel, in which a breve is simply broken down into as many equal parts as required.[2] As Bent argues, this is at odds with Jacobus's statement that Petrus 'followed' Franco as well as Jacobus's own conception of the perfect breve as strictly tripartite (such that only three and nine semibreves could be equal).

Bent also emphasises that, again according to Jacobus, the innovation of presenting more than three semibreves within the time of a perfect breve was not exclusive to Petrus. There was 'another' ('unus alius') who divided the breve into nine semibreves, trumping Petrus's maximum of seven.[3] And, confusingly, Jacobus also attributes to Franco himself the composition of a triplum that divided the breve into more than three semibreves. On this point, Jacobus is hesitant: it 'seems' ('videtur') to him that in Paris he heard such a triplum 'composed by Magister Franco, it was said' ('a magistro Francone, ut dicebatur'). It is unclear whether Franco's triplum adopted Petrus's innovations or (as suggested later in relation to the survival of one such motet in **Mo**'s old corpus) anticipated them. The attribution of such a triplum to Franco may rather have been purely political on Jacobus's part, intended to convey the authority and justifications of the ancients on Petrus's practice, in spite of the fact that it violated their laws.

In any case, Jacobus's account is contradictory. On the one hand, Petrus's contribution does not emerge from it as particularly significant: Petrus is not the most radical in his use of semibreves, nor (if indeed Franco did it before him) may he even be the first to exceed the division of the breve into three parts. Crucially, Petrus relies on a notational technique – the dot of division to mark individual breve units – that is also inherited from Franco.[4] On the other hand, Jacobus simultaneously asserts Petrus's status as the innovator who 'began' the practice of multiple semibreves. Moreover, and as David Maw notes, the opening of **Mo** 7 enacts the compositional chronology narrated by Jacobus: that Petrus first began to try out

2   Ibid., 39–43. See also Desmond 2018b, 127–30.
3   See Bent 2015, 32 on the possible identity of Jacobus's 'unus alius' as the Johannes de Garlandia cited by Handlo.
4   Franco stipulates that dots be used to clarify the groupings of semibreves into pairs and/or trios within a chain of successive semibreves. See Reaney and Gilles 1974, 39.

four-semibreve groups in *S'amours eust*, the triplum of the fascicle's first piece, and that he then went on to use groups of five, six, and seven semibreves in the triplum *Aucun ont trouve*, **Mo** 7's second motet.[5] Despite the suggestion that Franco himself also used more than three semibreves in the time of a breve, Jacobus named Petrus – rightly or not – as the instigator of this practice and traced its emergence across two of his compositions. That these two motets were placed at the head of the collection in **Mo** 7 confirms their and Petrus's importance.

Difficulties in Defining the 'Petronian' Motet

Fourteenth-century theorists do not explicitly specify that Petrus's semibreves were individually texted, but precisely such syllabic (rather than melismatic) semibreves and their notation distinguish the musical examples they cite.[6] Modern scholars have, therefore, retained an emphasis on syllabic semibreves in delimiting a corpus for or linked to Petrus, but even still there is a lack of consensus.[7] In total, there are nine different compositions in **Mo** fascicles 7 and 8 that divide their breves into more than three semibreves (see Table 4.1).[8] Maw considers all of these pieces to be compositions by Petrus himself, but Ernest Sanders and Peter M. Lefferts and Richard Crocker were more circumspect, excluding *Entre Jehan et Philippet/ Nus hom ne puet desiervir/CHOSE TASSIN* (**Mo** 7, no. 294), which stands out stylistically for its use of its fast-moving secular tenor.[9] Crocker also

---

5 Maw 2018, 179.
6 On theoretical citations of Petrus beyond Jacobus, see Bent 2015, 27–32.
7 Lefferts 1986, 76 and 79–80, describes the style of nine Latin-texted motets in English sources as 'Petronian'. However, not all of these pieces feature as many as four syllabic semibreves in the time of a breve (compare 96, Table 13) and for those that do, their semibreves – unlike those in **Mo** 7, 8 or **Tu** – are usually notated with stems (see 99). See also Desmond 2018a, 154–56 on **Onc**, and Desmond 2018c for an expanded overview of semibreve notation in England in this period. See also Catalunya 2017 for examples of Continental sources from the 1320s and 1330s containing both syllabic and melismatic (unstemmed) four-semibreve groups in Latin-texted tripla.
8 There are two further motets in **Mo** 7 that achieve four (principally melismatic) semibreves within the time of a perfect breve, but under different notational and stylistic circumstances. A decoration at the end of the triplum of no. 271 effectively creates a four-semibreve melisma through the ad hoc notation of a plicated *cum opposita proprietate* ligature immediately followed by a lone semibreve. As noted in Wolinski 1988, 131–33, motet no. 277 – a hocket in the sixth imperfect mode – features three-semibreve melismas within the time of an altered or 'major' semibreve (i.e. the equivalent of two *recta* or 'minor' semibreves), such that overall there are four semibreves (one syllabic, three melismatic) contained within a perfect breve unit.
9 See Maw 2018, 161–64; Ernest H. Sanders and Peter M. Lefferts, 'Petrus de Cruce', in *Grove Music Online*, https://doi.org/10.1093/gmo/9781561592630.article.21491 (accessed 20 Aug. 2021); Crocker 1990, 670 n. 50. I consider doubtful Maw's attribution to Petrus

Table 4.1 **Mo** 7 and 8 motets with four or more semibreves in the time of a perfect breve

Motet texts (in **Mo** order)	Concordances	≥ four semibreves in the time of a perfect breve	Attribution
S'amours eust/ Au renouveler/ ECCE [IAM] [M 61]	**Mo** 7, no. 253 **Tu**, no. 21	Syllabic 4-SB groups	Petrus
Aucun ont trouve/ Lonc tens/ ANNUN[TIANTES] [M 9]	**Mo** 7, no. 254 **Tu**, no. 11	Syllabic 5-, 6-, & 7-SB groups	Petrus
Aucuns vont souvent/ Amor, qui cor vulnerat/ KYRIEELEYSON [M 86d]	**Mo** 7, no. 264 **Tu**, no. 10 **Ca** (motetus and tenor only) **ArsC** (motetus text)	Syllabic 4-, 5-, & 6-SB groups	None
Amours, qui si me maistrie/ Solem iusticie/ SOLEM [O 19]	**Mo** 7, no. 289 Triplum revised in **Mo** 8, no. 338	Syllabic 4-SB groups & 6-SB group Syllabic 4-, 5-, & 6-SB groups	None
Entre Jehan et Philippet/ Nus hom ne puet desiervir/ CHOSE TASSIN [C]	**Mo** 7, no. 294	Syllabic 4-SB groups	None
Lonc tans ai/ Tant ai souffert/ SURREXIT [M 75]	**Mo** 7, no. 298	Single melismatic 4-SB group	None
Pour chou que j'aim/ Li jolis tans/ KYRIELEISON [M 86g]	**Mo** 7, no. 299	Syllabic 4-SB groups (and isolated melismatic 4-SB group in motetus)	None
Aucun, qui ne sevent servir/Iure tuis laudibus/ [VIRGO] MARIA [O 50]	**Mo** 8, no. 317	Syllabic 4-, 5-, & 6-SB groups	None
Je cuidoie bien metre/ Se j'ai folement ame/ SOLEM [O 19]	**Mo** 8, no. 332	Syllabic 4- & 5-SB groups	None

of **Mo** 7, no. 294. Maw admits that this piece is set apart stylistically – in its harmonic language and its rhythmically homogenous texture – from other 'Petronian' works (see 162), omitted *Lonc tans ai/Tant ai souffert/SURREXIT* (**Mo** 7, no. 298), whose triplum exceptionally employs only a single and melismatic four-semibreve decoration among its many pairs and trios of syllabic semibreves.[10] But he added four pieces that never exceed the division of the breve into three on the grounds of their stylistically similarity – rapidly syllabic tripla usually accompanied by slow-moving or unpatterned tenors – to works by Petrus.[11]

All of these categorisations carry their own problems. There are at least two further motets that do not exceed the division of the breve into three in **Mo** 7 and 8 that would merit inclusion in Crocker's stylistic corpus.[12] Within the circumscribed group of motets that use four or more syllabic semibreves, the fascicle 8 motet *Je cuidoie/Se j'ai folement/SOLEM* (no. 332) is an outlier in its frequent use of hockets and its modernity.[13] Any definition of 'Petronian' that rests purely on the number of semibreves, whether syllabic or melismatic, opens up the corpus to the inclusion of further compositions beyond **Mo**. There are four motets in **Tu** that include four-semibreve melismatic decorations absent from the concordances of the same pieces in **Mo**, and a motet in the fourteenth-century northern Italian manuscript **Ob E 42** with four-semibreve decorations that are absent from the contrafactum version of this motet in both **Mo** 7 and **Tu**.[14] Three unique fragmentary motets – two Latin pieces in **Stockholm** and one French one in **Leuven** – also employ four-semibreve melismatic turn figures within the context of motetus and triplum voices that otherwise divide their breves into a maximum of two texted semibreves.[15]

It seems that the addition of four-semibreve melismas in the late thirteenth and early fourteenth centuries became a fairly standard decorative convention, and one that could also be divorced from the syllabic declamation and rhythmic stratification of Petrus's motets. Notably, of the eight

---

and he also finds it difficult to accommodate within his chronological picture of Petrus's motets (see 180). Moreover, as outlined in Chapter 3, the relationship between Adam's *Entre Adam et Haniket* and the *Entre Jehan et Philippet* triplum suggests that the composer of this latter motet, participating in the tradition of self-naming, was a 'Jehan'.

10 **Mo** 7, no. 298 is the only motet in Sanders and Lefferts' corpus that is not attributed to Petrus in Tischler 1978.

11 These are **Mo** 7, nos. 255 and 297 and **Mo** 8, nos. 316 and 330.

12 Plausible additions to Crocker's corpus include **Mo** 7, no. 262 (also suggested by Maw 2018, 162 n. 5, and discussed later) and **Mo** 8, no. 311 (very similar in its triparte structure and use of hockets to **Mo** 8, no. 332).

13 Desmond 2018b, 15 n. 45, notes the 'Ars nova' character of **Mo** 8, no. 332.

14 On the **Tu** motets, see Johnson 1991, 559–600. The **Ob E 42** motet is a contrafactum of **Mo** 7, no. 257. On **Ob E 42**, see Gallo 1970.

15 On **Leuven**, see Kügle 1997b. On **Stockholm**, see Catherine A. Bradley, 'Perspectives for Lost Polyphony and Red Notation around 1300: Medieval Motet and Organum Fragments in Stockholm' (forthcoming). The notation of these four-semibreve melismas does not involve plicae or conjuncturae, but rather four distinct and separate diamond-shaped note heads which are nonetheless perceptible as a group.

(unique) motets in the first supplement of **Mo** 7, three (of which one, no. 294, has a fast-moving song tenor) divide their breves into as many as four semibreves (and only once and melismatically in no. 298), but none of the pieces in this supplement exceeds the division of the breve in four. **Mo** 7's first supplement seems to contain a distinct repertoire in which – unlike the main body of fascicle 7 and fascicle 8 – the use of four (syllabic or melismatic) semibreves within the time of a perfect breve seems to be the accepted maximum.[16] Probably in consequence, the scribe of the first supplement supplied dots of division to clarify chains of semibreve pairs, a technique also found in **Mo** 8 but not earlier in **Mo** 7, where the division of semibreves into groups of two was invariably the presumed default and did not need to be made explicit. The concentration in **Mo** 7's first supplement of motets on instrumental tenor melodies (three out of five examples in the fascicle as a whole, examined in Chapter 5) could be significant with regard to its treatment of semibreves: Anonymous IV, writing after Franco but in general describing much older forms of thirteenth-century notation and repertoire, several times states that the breve can be divided into two, three, or four.[17] These remarks apparently pertain to instrumental music, but if four-semibreve decorations were common in this context then their use in contemporary motets, especially within a group of pieces that included several built on instrumental melodies, might not be so remarkable.[18] These various circumstances – notational, practical, and theoretical – undermine the unassailable significance of three as the conventional maximum number of semibreves within the space of a breve.

Syllabic Semibreves Before Petrus

The theoretical three-semibreve watershed is further undermined by the fact that the majority of compositions in **Mo** 7 and **Mo** 8 do not actually divide their breves into more than *two* syllabic semibreves.[19] In this respect, **Mo** 7 and 8 reflect and preserve the established treatment of syllabic semibreves already evident in earlier sources such as **Mo**'s old corpus (dated around

---

16 The motetus **Mo** 7, no. 299, whose triplum features multiple syllabic four-semibreve groups, contains a single four-semibreve melisma that is otherwise entirely anomalous in the context of a motetus voice in **Mo**.

17 See discussion in Wolinski 1988, 133. On the date of Anonymous IV, see Wegman 2015, esp. 714–15.

18 See Desmond 2018b, 42.

19 See Desmond 2018a, 141 and 149–50. Her categorisation of fascicle 8 motets according to texture and rhythmic characteristics distinguishes as a group those motets with three or more texted semibreves, undermining the sharp stylistic distinction of motets that use four or more texted semibreves in the time of a breve.

1270), where breves never contain as many as three syllabic semibreves.[20] There is one exceptional composition, *Par une matinee/Mellis stilla/DOM-INO*, recorded in fascicle 3 of **Mo** (no. 40) and in **Cl**, which is remarkable in dividing its breves not only into three texted semibreves but also (on two occasions) into four.[21] Sean Curran has proposed that these four-semibreve groups – both reciting on a single pitch – express musically the text's declaration that a lover's lament has moved beyond the boundaries of sense and logic.[22] Such a textual motivation is highly probable. *Par une matinee* not only breaks with the two-semibreve convention in its use of syllabic three-semibreve groups but its use of four-semibreve groups renders it a Petronian motet *avant la lettre*. It has never yet been attributed to Petrus.

Could *Par une matinee* have been an early experiment by Petrus later unknown to Jacobus, who was either mistaken in asserting that *S'amour eust* was Petrus's first use of four-semibreve groups, or who cited *S'amour eust* because such four-semibreve groups were first properly established here and (unlike in *Par une matinee*) notated unambiguously through the use of clarificatory dots of division? Perhaps more likely, *Par une matinee* was the triplum said to be by Franco which Jacobus knew. New ground broken by *Par une matinee* may have instigated the theoretical justifications of a strictly triple conceptualisation of the breve by both Lambertus and Franco himself, rejecting the radical four-semibreve groups, whose disruptive existence could have been the impetus to set a maximum limit for the division of the breve. An extant theoretical reference to *Par une matinee* underlines its significance and supports this hypothesis. The triplum is named in the 1279 treatise by the St Emmeram Anonymous, which

---

20 On the use of syllabic semibreves in the old corpus, see Desmond 2018a, 152–53; Wolinski 1992, 289. Motets which use texted semibreves – and exclusively pairs (with the exception of no. 40) – number 32 out of 234 pieces in **Mo**'s old corpus: fascicle 2, nos. 23–24, 28, 31–32; fascicle 3, nos. 36–40 and 44; fascicle 4, nos. 52–53 and 59; fascicle 5, nos. 76–77, 84, 89, 100, 102–03, 108, 114, 119, 126, 129, 137, 143–44, 164, and 176; and fascicle 6, no. 217.

21 Ludwig 1978, 405–06, rejected these two four-semibreve groups in **Mo** as errors, on the grounds that such a division of the breve was not yet possible. Similarly, Tischler's 1978 edition of **Mo** 3, no. 40 (vol. 2, 13–15) corrected the original notation – reducing to a semibreve the breve following the four-semibreve group – to allow the two four-semibreves groups to occupy more than a single breve. The exact concordance for these four-semibreve passages in **Cl** – whose small and frequent textual and melodic variants demonstrate its textual independence from **Mo** – challenges the presumption that they must be erroneous. The analysis of *Par une matinee* in **Cl** in Curran 2013, 81–84, respects the original notation and takes seriously the need to accommodate these two four-semibreve groups within the breve unit. See also Curran 2013, 209–10 for a comparison of the **Mo** and **Cl** tripla. The motetus incipit *Mellis stilla maris* in the **Bes** table of contents (no. 2), alongside pieces for which only vernacular tripla survive, suggests that this source also preserved the *Par une matinee* triplum.

22 See Curran 2013, 168–92.

rebukes Lambertus and pre-dates Franco's *Ars cantus*. Discussing the concept of 'equivalence' ('aequipollentia'), in which individual notes can effectively be transposed both into longer or shorter rhythmic values, the St Emmeram Anonymous states that such conversion could be undertaken for 'all motets' ('omnes motellos') unless this is prevented by an 'excess of semibreves' ('semi-brevium superfluitas') caused by a 'superabundance of syllables' ('superhabun-dantiam litterae'), as 'evident in the motet *Par une matinee* and in others of this kind'.[23]

The St Emmeram Anonymous, in his reference to *Par une matinee*, may have considered its trios of syllabic semibreves excessive, just as well as its quadruplets. That he knew and identified *Par une matinee* as an example of textual superabundance is telling, but though notable, this triplum was evidently not the only such in circulation in 1279. The St Emmeram Anony-mous's reference to *Par une matinee* confirms that, if a triplum by Franco, its composition must indeed have pre-dated the completion of Franco's *Ars cantus*, at which point – and possibly in response to Lambertus's treatise – Franco evidently thought better of the four-semibreve groups. A subsequent rejection of the possibility of four syllabic semibreves within the time of a breve is borne out by alternative Latin contrafactum versions of the *Par une matinee* triplum in **PsAr** (*O maria mater pia*, in a musical appendix to a copy of Lambertus's treatise) and in **Ba** (*Virginis preconia*). Both Latin tripla nota-bly expunge the two syllabic four-semibreve groups, replacing them with rhythms that respect Lambertian and Franconian precepts. Whether *Par une matinee* was by Petrus, Franco, or someone else altogether, it use of four-semibreve groups – theoretically illicit by 1280 – seems to have been a largely isolated experiment that did not meet with immediate adoption elsewhere, and was not revived or reinvented by Petrus for probably a decade at least.

Ba and the table of contents which is all that remains of the **Bes** motet collection are the principal witnesses to a layer of the motet repertoire that straddles **Mo**'s old corpus and fascicle 7. Like the old corpus, but unlike fascicle 7, dots of division are not used in **Ba** to clarify breve units, and they are largely unnecessary here. Syllabic semibreves in **Ba** are invariably grouped in pairs, with the exception of just four out of the one hundred motets in this source, which divide their breves into as many as three texted semibreves. This indicates that motet tripla with as many as three texted semibreves were – even if the St Emmeram Anonymous knew several of them – probably still rare around 1280, and the polyphonic context in which such tripla appear is also significant. Three out of the four tripla to use as many as three texted semibreves in **Ba** were created in the same way: as

23 See full the text and translation (here adapted) of this passage in Yudkin 1985, 236–37.

additions to pre-existing two-voice motets, which had an independent and often long-established circulation of their own.[24] *Mellis stilla/DOMINO*, above which *Par une matinee* and its contrafacta were added, circulated more widely as a two-voice motet than with its multi-note tripla, while the lower voices of *Quant vient en mai/Ne sai que je die/IOHANNE* and *Dame de valour/He Dieus, quant je remir/AMO[RIS]* – both also copied in **Mo** 7 (nos. 274 and 281) – appear as two-voice motets in the earliest extant motet collection in **F** (dated in the 1240s).

Early examples of motet tripla that use as many as three syllabic semibreves, then, usually experimented above older, and apparently well-known, polyphonic foundations.[25] Remarkably, a unique motet in **Mo** 8 seems to celebrate precisely this compositional development and technique. Anne Ibos-Augé has recently demonstrated that the triplum of *Par une matinee/O clemencie/D'UN JOLI DART* (**Mo** 8, no. 309) is a patchwork of musical and textual quotations, all preserved earlier in **Mo**.[26] The incipit of the **Mo** 8 triplum adopts the complete first phrase of the exceptional old-corpus *Par une matinee* triplum. In the body of the fascicle 8 triplum follows a quotation of the first two phrases of the triplum *Dame de valour*, a reworking of an older polyphonic foundation and one of the few tripla in **Ba** to use as many as three syllabic semibreves (also recorded in **Bes**, **Mo** 7, and **Tu**). The **Mo** 8 motet's final extended quotation of music and text is, again, a complete triplum incipit.[27] The triplum of *Bien me doi/Je n'ai, que que/KYRIE FONS* (absent from **Ba**, but present in **Bes**, **Mo** 7, and **Tu**) features trios as well as pairs of syllabic semibreves, and was crafted above a motetus voice that had an independent existence as a monophonic song by Richard de Fournival, the Amiens trouvère who died in 1260.[28]

---

24 The exceptional fourth **Ba** motet is *De vois/He bone/APTATUR* (also in **Bes**), whose motetus and triplum are similar in rhythmic profile and were probably conceived together.

25 This practice is evident also the **Mo** 8 motet *Virginale/Descendi/ALMA [REDEMPTORIS MATER]* (no. 330, additionally preserved in **Da**), which adds a new declamatory-style triplum – with pairs and trios of texted semibreves – to an existing two-voice foundation. This foundation circulates as a two-voice motet in **ArsA** and **LoD**, and it is also associated with two different triplum texts and melodies that move at the same basic rate as their accompanying motetus: in **Ba** (*Gaude super omina*) and in **Mo** 7 and **LoHa** (*Anima mea liquefacta*).

26 Ibos-Augé 2018a, 212–19, identifies these quotations and discusses their textual significance.

27 An earlier, much shorter music-and-text quotation in this **Mo** 8 triplum – the first six notes of the motetus incipit 'Li dous pensers', **Mo** 7, no. 280 – does not involve syllabic semibreves. Perhaps the refrain cento tenor of no. 280 itself inspired its quotation in another cento.

28 See Robert Falk and John Haines, 'Richard de Fournival', in *Grove Music Online* (accessed 30 Aug. 2020), https://doi.org/10.1093/gmo/9781561592630.article.23391. *Je n'ai, que que* appears within an early fourteenth-century treatise on love, *Le commens d'amours*, uniquely preserved in **Dijon** 526 (fol. 9v), where space is left for a single line of melody

The patchwork triplum of *Par une matinee/O clemencie/D'UN JOLI DART* might narrate early developments in the syllabic semibreve style, apparently presenting its quotations in chronological order and here in virtuosic combination with a fast-moving vernacular song quotation in the tenor. That the cento starts with the **Mo** 3 triplum *Par une matinee*, linking it with other syllabic tripla recorded in **Mo** 7, underlines the significance and subsequent appreciation in practice of this radical old-corpus motet, possibly by Franco himself. The fascicle 8 cento seems to document a moment before the advent of Petrus's *S'amours eust* or *Aucun ont trouve*, when trios of texted semibreves were still new and rare and five-, six- or seven-semibreve groups were not yet in use. Of course, Petrus could have created syllabic tripla using only pairs and trios of semibreves both before and indeed after the composition of *S'amours eust* and *Aucun ont trouve*. It is therefore possible that Petrus was the composer of material quoted in fascicle 8's *Par une matinee* triplum and even of this (self-fashioning?) cento itself. If the triplum's opening quotation, *Par une matinee*, was from Franco this would have been an appropriate reflection of his theoretical authority and of his emphasis on the tripartite division of the breve, perhaps first practised in the syllabic semibreves of this particular triplum (although problematically also exceeded by its two quadruple semibreve groups). Alternatively, the **Mo** 8 motet could have been a later and pointed attempt to retell the story of rhythmic innovations that had come to be linked to Petrus, deliberately eschewing any quotation of Petrus's famous compositions and opening with *Par une matinee* precisely because it anticipated *S'amours eust*.

Petrus and 'Petronian' Pieces in Context

Fascicle 8's patchwork *Par une matinee* triplum itself illustrates the fundamental complexity of categorising 'Franconian' and 'Petronian' semibreves: it serves to foreground an exceptional and apparently avant-garde old corpus motet (possibly by Franco himself) that exceeds the division of the breve in three, while continuing to quote from subsequent compositions (some potentially by Petrus) that respected this limit. Various other, less explicit, intertextual connections likewise serve to undermine any sense of a paradigm shift in the treatment of syllabic semibreves, with Franco and Petrus, respectively, on either side of a three-semibreve divide. This is not to deny internal connections

---

for which staves and notation were never entered. **Dijon 526** does not name Richard as the author of this treatise (or song) but several other works in this manuscript with external ascriptions Richard are here anonymous (see Langlois 1904, 105–10; Saly 1972), and Richard's authorship of *Je n'ai, que que* is accepted (see, for example, Saint-Cricq 2019, 194). On the interpretative context of this song in *Le commens d'amours* and as part of its three-voice motet, see Thomson 2018, 248–53.

evident between compositions in Table 4.1 where the use of many texted semi-breves is clearly a priority: Petrus's *Aucun ont trouve*, itself a quotation of Adam's *Aucun se sont loe*, surely prompted the use of this same initial word in two further motets that divided their breves into as many as six semibreves. Likewise, it cannot be coincidental that two separate motets that exceed the division of the breve into four adopt the otherwise obscure tenor SOLEM.[29] However, while two 'Petronian' motets in **Mo** 7 share the relatively unusual use of Kyrie melodies as their tenors there are three further KYRIE tenor motets in this fascicle with declamatory 'Franconian' tripla, two of which are closely linked with 'Petronian' compositions.[30]

Mo 7 prominently presents Petrus's *S'amours eust* and *Aucun ont trouve* as a pair, but **Tu** – the only other manuscript to preserve these pieces in full – does not.[31] In **Tu** there is instead an internal group of three motets on KYRIE tenors followed by two 'Aucun' motets that are separated in **Mo** 7.[32] *Bien me doi/Je n'ai, que que/KIRIE FONS* (**Tu**, no. 8), *J'ai mis toute/Je n'en puis/PUERORUM* (**Tu**, no. 9), and *Aucuns vont souvent/Amor, qui cor vulnerat/KYRIE ELEYSON* (**Tu**, no. 10) appear side by side in **Tu**, imme-diately followed by *Aucun ont trouve* (no. 11).[33] *Aucuns vont souvent* uses up to six syllabic semibreves and Petrus's neighbouring *Aucun ont trouve* reaches seven. The first two motets on KYRIE tenors – also presented as a pair in **Bes** – likewise make heavy use of syllabic semibreves in their tripla (especially *J'ai mis toute ma pensee*), but only of pairs and trios.[34] Never-theless, these three KYRIE tenor motets share their tenor design: all state

---

29 The SOLEM tenor is otherwise extant in one other motet in the thirteenth-century reper-toire, the widely transmitted and possibly English composition *Iam (iam) nubes/Iam (iam) novum/SOLEM*, which is also recorded in the main body of **Mo** 7 (no. 275).

30 A total of just ten different motets (none found in sources earlier than c.1270) employ Kyrie melodies as their tenors. One further KYRIE tenor motet in **Mo** 7 (no. 286) is in an older, modal style.

31 *Aucun ont trouve* is the eleventh motet in **Tu**, while *S'amours eust* is the twenty-first.

32 The alternative ordering in **Mo** 7 nonetheless bears out, in a different way, connections between 'Aucun' openings, KYRIE tenors, and a certain proximity to Adam and Petrus. In **Mo** 7, the KYRIE tenor motet *J'ai mis toute ma pensee* (no. 255) directly follows (rather than indirectly preceding, as in **Tu**) *Aucun ont trouve* (no. 254), while *Aucuns vont souvent* (no. 264) follows Adam's *Aucun se sont loe* (no. 263), which is itself preceded by *Bien me doi* (no. 262).

33 I am not convinced by the identification in Johnson 1991, 560–67, of the tenor of *Aucuns vont/Amor, qui cor/KYRIE ELEYSON* as a local Amiens version of its Kyrie chant. John-son's 'Amiens' version of the chant is distinguished only by the presence of a single pass-ing note, shared by the motet tenor but absent from a Parisian copy of the same chant (see the melodic comparison on 563). Moreover, the Amiens Kyrie introduces an extra repeated note absent from both the Parisian version of the chant and the motet tenor.

34 **Bes** contained *Bien me doi/Je n'ai, que que/KIRIE FONS* (as no. 24) followed by *J'ai mis toute/Je n'en puis/PUERORUM* (no. 25).

their (different) tenor melodies twice, rhythmicised as a unbroken string of perfect longs.[35] As noted earlier, the motetus *Je n'ai, que que* is a song attributed to Richard de Fournival, and the motetus of its neighbouring composition, *Je n'en puis*, also had an independent transmission as a ballette in **Douce 308**.[36] Its concluding phrases apart, *Je n'ai, que que* is consistent in its use of eight- and seven-syllable lines and four-perfection phrases, while *Je n'en puis* (again with the exception of its last line and a single intrusive 'Dieus' exclamation) proceeds in regular ten-syllable lines and five-perfection phrases. The Latin motetus of the final KYRIE tenor motet, *Amor, qui cor vulnerat*, is similarly regular, with consistent seven-syllable lines and four-perfection phrases, a regularity common also to two further motetus voices in 'Petronian' compositions in **Mo** 7 and 8.[37] *Amor, qui cor vulnerat/ KYRIE* survives as a two-voice motet, without its vernacular triplum, in **Ca** and **ArsC**, confirming that it too had an independent and probably pre-existing status. In any case, the three KYRIE tenor motets clearly respond to one another in their choice and arrangement of tenor chants, revealing a shared preference for regular motetus voices, often song quotations, and borrowed foundations to support their declamatory tripla.

This interlinked group of 'Franconian' and 'Petronian' motets in **Tu** highlights the danger of isolating compositions that divide their breve into four or more semibreves as a self-contained corpus. Paradoxically, there is also external evidence to suggest that the two works in this particular group whose semibreves do not exceed three per breve could be by Petrus. Petrus may have been behind the quotation of a song by Richard de Fournival, a former chancellor of Amiens Cathedral, in *Bien me doi/Je n'ai, que que/KYRIE FONS*.[38] The related *J'ai mis toute/Je n'en puis/PUERORUM*, too, points north of Paris. Its tenor text, the rare Kyrie trope *Puerorum caterva*, is – as both Ludwig and Rokseth noted – known principally from northern French and English manuscripts, and is less prevalent than the *Rex splendens* trope

---

35 This tenor structure is shared also by the unique KYRIE tenor motet in the first supplement to fascicle 7 that uses syllabic four-semibreve groups, *Pour chou/Li jolis tans, que/ KYRIELEISON*.

36 See the edition in Doss-Quinby and Rosenberg 2006, 320–22, no. 110. In the context of **Douce 308** ballettes, *Je n'en puis* (RS 726) is exceptional in its single-stanza form and lack of a clear refrain (see Doss-Quinby and Rosenberg 2006, xciv).

37 Maw 2018, 174 n. 33 also noted the poetic regularity of *Amor, qui cor vulnerat* as well as of motetus voices in two further 'Petronian' compositions: *Tant ai souffert* (**Mo** 7, no. 298), which alternates seven- and eight-syllable lines over phrases of four perfections, and *Iure tuis laudibus* (**Mo** 8, no. 317), with consistent seven-syllable lines and four-perfection phrases.

38 Maw 2018, 162 n. 5, noting that this motet could have been included in Crocker's list of 'Petronian'-style pieces, acknowledged that an ascription to Richard de Fournival 'need not count against Petrus's composition, as both men had links with Amiens'.

associated with the same melody.[39] While the earliest (eleventh- and twelfth-century) sources of the *Puerorum caterva* trope are from Cambrai, its appearance in a fifteenth-century printed missal of Amiens indicates that this was a text with which Petrus may well have been familiar.[40] In this regard, it is suggestive that the vernacular song tenor accompanying the **Mo** 8 triplum *Par une matinee*, with its patchwork of quotations from early experiments in syllabic tripla (including *Bien me doi*), names a location (Compiègne) in Picardy, between Amiens and Paris. Tellingly, **Mo** 7's first supplement also was singled out by Rokseth for its concentration of motets with traces of Picard dialect, a pronounced feature of Petrus's two known compositions as well.[41] As suggested earlier, the use of groups of four (but not more) semibreves within the time of a breve seems to be in more standard use in this supplement than in the fascicle's main body. This could indicate that the locus of interest in declamatory, multi-note vernacular tripla, including those which did not exceed the division of the breve in three or capped this division at four, lay north of Paris, and perhaps prominently with Petrus.

Conclusions

This chapter has, to some extent, played devil's advocate with the question of a corpus for Petrus. It has queried the significance in practice of a three-semibreve watershed and the necessity of a direct connection to Petrus for motets that exceed this limit, while conversely positing possible links to Petrus for motets that do not. Any attempt to pin down Petrus's rhythmic techniques and/or style in order to identify a discrete and definitive body of his compositions is arguably as impossible as it is unproductive. Nevertheless, Petrus's contemporary importance and the peculiarity of his known compositions usefully open up questions about the distinctiveness and personal identity of a compositional voice. Maw has characterised Petrus's musical and poetic expression as individualised, immediate, and self-consciously novel, and so perhaps inherently unsuited to widespread adoption by others.[42] It is true that declamatory tripla (including those that do not exceed the division of the breve in three) are distinctive, not to say bizarre, and they remain in somewhat limited phenomenon,

---

39 See Ludwig 1978, 427; Rokseth 1935–39, vol. 4, 187. The exceptional lack of the usual preface KYRIE for this tenor – which is designated simply PUERORUM, PUERORUM CATERVA, and PUERORUM TENOR in **Mo**, **Tu**, and **Ca** respectively – may reflect the fact that scribes did not identify this relatively obscure text as a KYRIE trope.

40 See Blume and Bannister 1905, 89.

41 Rokseth 1935–39, vol. 4, 79 and 274.

42 See Maw 2018, esp. 181–83. Maw's 'lexicon' of Petronian groups (166–68) draws exclusively on **Mo**, without consideration of variants in **Tu** or of other 'Petronian' groups present in compositions outside his corpus (such as in **Tu**, **Ob E 42**, **Leuven**, and now **Stockholm**).

even within the broader context of **Mo** 7 and 8, which also include Latin motets where semibreve declamation does not feature at all. Extant French-texted tripla employing four or more syllabic semibreves are largely unique to **Mo** and do not survive at all beyond **Mo** and **Tu**. This could be thanks to their musical and textual extravagance, which would have required expert performance to be effective. Jacobus described Petrus as a 'worthy singer': did Petrus create soloistic tripla for himself to sing, a practice that went hand in hand with his self-reflective trouvère-like first-person texts which discuss singing and song?

Yet Jacobus's testimony also reveals that Petrus was not the sole practitioner of the declamatory semibreve style, since 'another' created tripla in the same, indeed more radical, vein. However significant, Petrus's cannot have been a lone voice. Moreover, within the vernacular repertoire of **Mo** 7 and 8 more broadly – not confined to triplum voices or to motets by Petrus and/or in a declamatory semibreve style – rhetorical self-reflections in the first-person on the inspiration for and acts of song-making take over from the standard courtly and pastourelle texts more prominent in **Mo**'s old corpus.[43] Late thirteenth-century motets in **Mo** 7 and 8 betray a more personalised form of text expression and (sometimes) a more soloistic musical style at the same time as a more evident preoccupation with their musical community (as outlined in Chapter 3), and a continued and intense emphasis on quotation and cross-reference.

An interest in community is not antithetical to a sense of individual identity and might, in fact, heighten it. If virtuosic tripla are added to historical foundations the fact that this older lower-voice material is borrowed – and/ or it is musically and textually regular and predictable – may place the emphasis all the more strongly on the novelty of the added top voice and the identity of its composer or performer. Similarly, play with various internal musical and textual characteristics, techniques, and conventions – such as opening words or types of tenor chant and arrangement – can take the form of self-reference and perhaps self-aggrandisement, but external quotations (as in the case of Petrus's quotation of Adam at the outset of *Aucun ont trouve*) also serve as self-positioning. Practitioners of distinctive declamatory tripla may have been a relatively modest group of skilled proponents, of which Petrus was an influential member. In this context, the names of individual singers and composers were surely known, and a sense of their identity and position only enhanced by others whose styles they chose to invoke or imitate.

---

43 Multiple texts in **Mo** 7 and 8 reflect on singing and its motivations in their opening phrase (often in some permutation of 'Se je chant', as in the motetus voices of **Mo** 7, nos. 255 and 277 and the tripla of **Mo** 8, nos. 311 and 316). Besseler 1927, 164 also identified this as the dominant thematic and rhetorical trend of late thirteenth-century French motet texts.

5   Non-Plainchant Tenor Quotations

Unwritten Songs and Questions of Compositional Ownership

In Chapter 4 I discussed motets with elaborate and densely syllabic vernacular tripla, usually supported by slow-moving and often freely rhythmicised plainchant tenors. This chapter turns to a contrasting group of late thirteenth-century compositions – of which **Mo** 7 and 8 likewise record almost the entire known repertoire – that takes as its tenors, not liturgical melodies, but secular ones. Such motets typically preserve the original rhythms of their secular tenor melodies, which move at a similar rate to their upper voices, thus altering somewhat the compositional parameters of motet composition. Whereas pre-existing chant melodies were rhythmically arranged at will to serve as the foundation of a motet, secular tunes usually came with and retained a pre-determined rhythmic profile. These non-liturgical tenors were most often a vernacular song or refrain melody accompanied by its French text. But there are also several apparently instrumental or newly composed motet tenors, which receive labels of various sorts but are never accompanied by syllabic texts (or any indications of a sacred or Latin-texted source). In this chapter I define and analyse a corpus of late thirteenth-century motets on non-plainchant tenors, not only within the context of **Mo** but also in other contemporary sources of both Continental and English provenance. I argue that these largely unique secular tenors offer a significant notated witness to the kinds of melodies and songs that were not usually or otherwise written down. Ultimately, I reflect on the implications for concepts of authorship and identity of exchanging long-established plainchant tenor melodies for vernacular songs and instrumental tunes.

Instrumental Tenors

The use of apparently instrumental melodies for four motets in **Mo** 7 has long been recognised.[1] These tenor melodies are labelled in the vernacular

---

1   On the estampie-like nature of CHOSE TASSIN tenors, see Aubry 1907, 32–34; Rokseth 1935–39, vol. 4, 203–04; McGee 1990, 17–18. On the group of instrumental CHOSE TASSIN and LOYSET tenors, see Everist 2018, 28–29.

DOI: 10.4324/9781003259282-6

by the names of their creators, with the prefix 'chose' ('thing').[2] There are three unique motets – one in the fascicle's main body and two in its first supplement – on three different melodies captioned CHOSE TASSIN; a further unique motet in the first supplement is on a tenor marked CHOSE LOYSET. As discussed in Chapter 3, Tassin has been identified by Yvonne Rokseth with a minstrel listed in royal accounts for 1288, and with the Tassinus mentioned by the theorist Johannes de Grocheio as a creator of estampies.[3] Loyset's identity is elusive, but the fact that his melody is labelled in the same way as Tassin's indicates that he was also an instrumentalist.[4]

In addition to these four well-known examples, a further unicum in the main part of fascicle 7 (no. 267) also merits consideration in this context.[5] This tenor is labelled simply 'L', a decorated initial for which the remainder of the text was never added, the only example of such an omission in the entire fascicle. In 1939, Rokseth questioned the still current expansion of this tenor text as 'LEYSON', established by Friedrich Ludwig, on the grounds of a loose resemblance to a Kyrie melody.[6] She noted that the tenor's fast-moving rhythmic profile looked more like the *punctum* of an estampie. L – which is just eight pitches in length and four perfections in duration, and is effectively a decorated cadence on a, repeated fourteen times to form a motet tenor – closely resembles several other secular tenors in **Mo** 7 (see Example 5.1).[7] The most extensive match is actually with the opening of the song tenor JE LA TRUIS TROP ASPRETE of a unique motet (no. 295) in fascicle 7's first supplement, in close proximity to two of the pieces on CHOSE TASSIN tenors and the CHOSE LOYSET motet. The first seven pitches of JE LA TRUIS TROP ASPRETE (marked by a box in Example 5.1) are identical – in pitch and rhythm – with all but L's final note.

---

2   The **Mo** unicum no. 49 included in the additions to fascicle 3 (considered to be contemporaneous with fascicle 7) also labels its tenor with a name, but without the prefix 'chose'. The tenor SOIER apparently names the same Sohiers the cooper whose exploits are described in the accompanying motetus text *A Cambrai avint l'autrier*. This melody could be instrumental: it is in ABB form and, in common with CHOSE LOYSET, features multiple iterations of an individual pitch (here F).

3   Rokseth 1935–39, vol. 4, 290.

4   Ibid., 295. Rokseth describes the CHOSE LOYSET tenor as the *punctum* of an estampie, designated by the name of a still unidentified musician.

5   A further candidate for an instrumental tenor is found in **Mo**'s old corpus, in the unique fascicle 5 motet *Blanchete commme fleur/Quant je pens/VALARE* (no. 168). The mysteriously labelled and otherwise unknown VALARE tenor alternates downward leaps of a fourth (b flat – F) with scalic descending figures that fill in this same this same fourth outline.

6   See Rokseth 1935–39, vol. 4, 188; Ludwig 1978, 434–35. The expansion of the tenor as LEYSON (M86e) is accepted in van der Werf 1989, 96; Tischler 1978, vol. 3, 89.

7   Four iterations of the L figure are altered: three internal and successive statements include two extra presentations of the first two notes (followed by rests), and the tenor's closing statement adds two concluding perfect longs to cadence on F.

Wider comparison with the instrumental melodies CHOSE TASSIN and LOYSET reveals, however, that this figuration was something of a standard decoration (see boxed passages in Example 5.1).

The first [A] of the CHOSE TASSIN tenors, in **Mo** no. 270, contains a phrase whose opening three-note figure and final pitch are identical with L, but whose decorative semibreve figure turns in different direction and is pitched a third higher (on c). The CHOSE LOYSET melody – a pair of open and closed phrases (marked A and B) – twice presents just L's four-note decoration on the same pitch, a, as in L. And this same turn figure also appears twice in the CHOSE TASSIN [C] tenor, in **Mo** no. 294, first on F and then, again, on a. Only the second CHOSE TASSIN [B] motet, **Mo** no. 292, has a tenor that is substantially different in its rhythmic and melodic character (see the final system of Example 5.1). Here the interest seems to lie instead in frequent shifts between rhythmic modes one and two, although a lone three-breve leaping gesture (up to c and down to G) is shared with the opening of the earlier CHOSE TASSIN [A] tenor (marked by dashed boxes in Example 5.1). It is possible that this leaping figure may have been a consistent feature of Tassin's style. In general, Tassin's three melodies are longer and more unpredictable than the simple paired phrases of the tenor attributed to Loyset.

Although the L tenor is noticeably shorter than any of the melodies linked to either Tassin or Loyset, this melody is of their same secular musical cast, rather than that of liturgical plainchant. Despite L's close connection to the song melody *Je la truis trop asprete*, the prevalence of aspects of L's short phrase in the CHOSE TASSIN and LOYSET tenors, and its consistency of pitch level, could indicate an instrumental context, in which the fast-moving decoration was compatible with certain fingering patterns. L could be tentatively expanded as LOYSET, but is difficult to explain why the prefix 'chose' would then have been omitted, and why Loyset's name – known to the scribe of fascicle 7's first supplement – escaped the copyist of this earlier layer. More probably, the generic and ubiquitous nature of the brief L tenor indicates that it was not a genuine quotation of a particular song or melody but rather a polyphonic elaboration of a stock musical gesture in general circulation. This would account for L's lack of tenor label, since any kind of associated text or attribution for such a generic phrase would not have been apposite.

L might be compared in this regard with two tenors in **Mo** 8 that are simply identified in the manuscript as 'tenor'.[8] As Oliver Huck observes,

---

8 Just one further motet foundation in fascicle 8 is labelled simply 'tenor'. The tenor of **Mo** 8, no. 322 (*Marie assumptio/Huius chori/TENOR*), is apparently a newly created melody, comprised of three different melodic components in rhythmically varied arrangements. As discovered by Anderson 1969, 230, the first 12 notes of the tenor match the PORTARE melisma exactly. However, the tenor then continues differently and its further two melodic *colores* are not related to the PORTARE plainchant. The rhythmicisation of the first part

Example 5.1 The L tenor, comparable secular melodies, and instrumental tenors in **Mo 7**

this is a designation never used in fascicle 7 or in **Tu**, and is more common in sources dated after 1300.[9] Both of the **Mo** 8 melodies labelled 'tenor' are very simple, repetitive musical foundations: the lowest voice of **Mo** 8, no. 314 (*Dieus, comment/Vo vair oel/TENOR*) oscillates between two prolonged pitches – its final, C, and D – while the musical basis of **Mo** 8, no. 328 (*Amor potest/Ad amorem/TENOR*) continually cycles around three notes, E, G, and its final, F. It could be that such tenors were indeed the sorts of underlying figurations usually played by instruments. They might equally have replicated the kinds of simple, newly composed foundations over which instrumental and/or vocal polyphony was generally improvised in practice. These fascicle 8 tenors are even less distinctive than L, and it is improbable that they could have been associated with particular musicians. The label 'tenor' – and the equivalent label 'pes' ('foot') for the similar kinds of simple musical foundations employed in motets in contemporary English sources – maintains the convention that the lowest voices of motets should receive an accompanying legend. The descriptive functional labels 'tenor' and 'pes' serve where any other accompanying text would be unnecessary or irrelevant, since the motet's foundational voice does not have any meaningful status as a quotation.

Vernacular Song Tenors in Continental Sources

Tenor identification is more straightforward for those motets that retain the convention of quotation and adopt song or refrain melodies as their lowest voices (listed in Table 5.1). The earliest surviving record of such a motet is the unique version of *Je ne puis/Flor de lis/DOUCE DAME QUE J'AIM TANT* in **Mo** 5, probably one of the newest motets in the old corpus, in the sixth imperfect mode (sometimes transcribed as duple meter) and with a triplum featuring pairs of syllabic semibreves.[10] Otherwise song-tenor motets

---

of the melody is not dissimilar in effect to the CHOSE TASSIN [A] and LOYSET tenors. Moreover, both second and third *colores* start with the same c-G-c figure as CHOSE TASSIN [A]. Whether of chant or instrumental origin, or a free reworking of a melody that deliberately combined aspects of both, the label 'tenor' seems to reflect difficulties in categorising this motet foundation.

9 Huck 2018, 97–99.

10 See Wolinski 2018, 191–92. The tenor of another unique old-corpus motet – *La jolivete/Douce amiete/V* (**Mo** 5, no. 175) – is melodically identical to the song tenor QUI PRENDROIT A SON CUER, used in two different motets in fascicle 7. The identity of the tenor of **Mo** 5, no. 175, which does not feature any texted semibreves, was not known to the scribe, who did not supply its accompanying song text. Instead, the tenor received only a decorative initial 'V', suggesting that it was mistaken for the widely used chant melisma VERITATEM, whose first three notes (F – G – a) share the same contour as the song tenor's first ordo (here G – a – b).

Table 5.1 Thirteenth- and early fourteenth-century motets in Continental sources with French-texted song or refrain tenors

Song tenor (in manuscript order)	Motet concordances (* indicates tenor texted in full)	Song or refrain concordances (attributions indicated in **bold**, where known; **Douce 308** = text only)	Musical form (the presence of a refrain text as well as melody is, when verifiable, indicated by capital letters)	Observations
DOUCE DAME QUE J'AIM TANT	**Mo** 5, no. 164 (alternative, unidentified tenor PROH DOLOR in **Ba**, no. 35)	**Douce 308** Ballette (RS 356)	ab ab	?Repetition of an opening phrase or a refrain.[11] b shares a opening, leading to different cadence
V = QUI PRENDROIT A SON CUER = QUI PRANDROIT	**Mo** 5, no. 175 (on G) **Mo** 7, no. 277 (on F) **Mo** 7, no. 302 (on F) (2nd supplement)	– 	4 × AB 3 × AB 3 × AB	?Repetition of a refrain
BELE YSABELOS	**Mo** 7, no. 256 **Tu**, no. 16 **Ba***, no. 52 **Bes**, no. 30	–	AB ab' ab' cc' b'B AB	Virelai-rondeau hybrid. Non-refrain derived material, but internal recapitulation of refrain text and melody for B material. c begins 5th higher (on d) than A and B (on G)
JOLIETEMENT	**Mo** 7, no. 260 **Tu**, no. 20 **Ba***, no. 53 **Bes**, no. 32 **Douce 139***	Refrain (vdB 1166) in *L'Abeïe du chastel amoureus* (text only) and *Renart le nouvel* (text and music)	AB aA ab AB	Conventional rondeau
HE RESVEILLE TOI	**Mo** 7, no. 269 **Bes**, no. 31	Refrain (vdB 870) in Adam de la Halle, *Jeu de Robin*	AB aa	Conventional rondeau. B has internal bb' form

NUS N'IERT JA JOLIS	Mo 7, no. 271 **Reg**	Polyphonic rondeau in **PaB** (text only)	AB aA ab AB	Conventional rondeau
CIS A CUI JE SUI AMIE	Mo 7, no. 272 **Wilh** (motetus only)	**Douce 308** Ballette (RS 1105)	6 × AB	Repetition of a refrain. b shares a opening, leading to different cadence
CIS A CUI . . . VOUS LE ME DEFENDES	Mo* 7, no. 280 Tu*, no. 23 Ba*, no. 54 **Bes**, no. 29	Opening = refrain of **Douce 308** Ballette (RS 1105) & external concordances for 5 further refrains	refrain cento	*Cis a cui* is initial quotation in a cento of 9 refrains
HE DAME JOLIE	Mo 7, no. 290	**Cgc 11** (text only) **Douce 308** Ballette (RS 1168) Refrain (vdB 806) in *Renart le noavel* (text and music) and in Anglo-Norman love letter in **CgC 54** (text only)	AB cc ab AB	Conventional virelai (AbbaA). B shares A opening, leading to different cadence. c begins with 5th leap (D – a)
JE LA TRUIS TROP ASPRETE	Mo 7, no. 295 (1st supplement)	**Douce 308** Ballette (RS 977)	AB cc ab AB	Conventional virelai (AbbaA). B shares A opening, leading to different cadence. Repeated-note phrase openings

11 The motet tenor text corresponds not to the refrain text of the **Douce 308** ballette but to the opening of its first stanza. See Doss-Quinby and Rosenberg 2006, no. 20, 62–64.

(*Continued*)

Table 5.1 (Continued)

Song tenor (in manuscript order)	Motet concordances (* indicates tenor texted in full)	Song or refrain concordances (attributions indicated in bold, where known; **Douce 308** = text only)	Musical form (the presence of a refrain text as well as melody is, when verifiable, indicated by capital letters)	Observations
D'UN JOLI DART	**Mo** 8, no. 309	**Douce 308** Pastourelle (RS 1256) Refrain (vdB 633) in *Renart le nouvel* (text and music)	refrain a a b refrain	*Pedes cum cauda*-virelai hybrid. *D'un joli dart* refrain frames *Defors compiegne* song in *pedes cum cauda* form. b shares refrain cadence. repeated-note phrase openings
= DEFORS COMPIEGNE	**Mo** 8, no. 321		a a b refrain	*Pedes cum cauda*-ballade hybrid. *Defors compiegne* song in *pedes cum cauda* form with concluding *D'un joli dart* refrain. = form of **Douce 308** pastourelle
J'AI FAIT TOUT NOUVELETEMENT (Refrain, vdB 934, quoted also in *La mesnie fauveline/J'ai fait nouveletement/ GRANT DESPIT*, **Fauv**)	**Mo** 8, no. 312	–	AB aa ab ab	Conventional rondeau.
VILAIN, LIEVE SUS O	**Mo** 8, no. 313	–	Ab c ab	Virelai (?AbA). Repeated-note phrase openings

NE ME BLASMES MIE	**Mo** 8, no. 318 **Tu,** no. 30	—	Ab bb ab ab	Rondeau form. bb for aa in second couplet
FRESE NOUVELE (Quoted also between upper-voices of *Je comence/Et je feray /SOULES VIEX:* **Ivrea, Add. 41667, Trémoille**)	**Mo*** 8, no. 319	—	4 × ab	Repetition of street cry
NON VEUL MARI	**Mo** 8, no. 323	—	Ab a'a' ab	Virelai (?AbA). New internal material is refrain-derived. a and b begin with 5th leap (D – a)
HE MI ENFANT	**Mo** 8, no. 325	—	Ab a'a' ab	Virelai (?AbA). New internal material is refrain-derived. Repeated-note phrase openings
RIENS NE VOUS VAUT	**Mo** 8, no. 333	—	Ab cc ab ab	Conventional virelai (?AbbaA). b shares a opening, leading to different cadence. c begins with 5th leap (F – c). Repeated-note phrase openings

(Continued)

Table 5.1 (Continued)

Song tenor (in manuscript order)	Motet concordances (* indicates tenor texted in full)	Song or refrain concordances (attributions indicated in bold, where known; **Douce 308** = text only)	Musical form (the presence of a refrain text as well as melody is, when verifiable, indicated by capital letters)	Observations
LONC TANS (= motetus of **Mo** 5, no. 78)	**Mo** 8, no. 337	–	through composed	Motetus voice. Opening material – twice repeated in a varied form – begins with 5th leap (D – a)
ORENDROIT PLUS	**Tu***, no. 15 **Arras frag.**	**Trouv. R** (text and music) **Douce 308** *Grand chant* (RS 197)	A a b	*Pedes cum cauda.* a has an internal ab form
QUANT LA SAISONS DESIREE[2]	**Tu***, no. 15 **Arras frag.**	**Trouv. R** (text and music) **Douce 308** *Grand chant* (RS 505)	A a b	*Pedes cum cauda.* a has an internal ab form
JE NE CHAINDRAI MAIS	**Tu**, no. 26 **Ivrea**, no. 38 **CaB** **Udine**	–	AB aA ab AB	Conventional rondeau (confirmed by text for ABaA extant in **Ivrea**)

				Motetus voice
LIS NE GLAI NE ROSIER FLOURI (= motetus of **Mo** 7, no. 266)	**Tu**, no. 28 (Initial 'L' but tenor otherwise untexted and notes ligated)	–	through composed	?*Pedes cum cauda*-virelai hybrid. a begins with 5th leap (D – a)
[] Tenor of *Clap, clap/ Sus Robin*	**Ivrea**, no. 80	–	refrain aab refrain aab refrain aab refrain	

12 In **Tu**, this voice occupies the manuscript position of the motetus. Visually, the tenor is another fully French-texted voice, *Qui bien aime a tart*, which opens with a refrain (vdB 1585). This refrain has multiple concordances, the majority of which are purely textual, and three additional extant melodies for vdB 1585 all differ from each other and from the melody in **Tu** (van der Werf 1989, 138, states incorrectly that the *Qui bien aime* text in **Tu** matches the first verse of a chanson attributed to Moniot d'Arras in **Vat**). Leach has convincingly proposed that functionally, in terms of range, and given its quotational nature, QUANT LA SAISONS DESIREE should be considered the motet tenor. See Leach 2015, 242–45, esp. 242 n. 60.

are principally to be found in **Mo**'s final fascicles, with ten in fascicle 7 – eight in the main body and one each in the first and second supplements – and ten more in **Mo** 8. The turn-of-the-century manuscript **Tu** is the next most substantial witness to this motet type, with eight examples in total, of which four are not also found in **Mo**. Yet, in general, song-tenor motets are not widely attested and most of the surviving examples are known only from a single source.[13]

The songs quoted as tenors in these motets are themselves also a largely unique repertoire. Just eleven of the twenty-four different vernacular tenors employed in Continental sources from the late thirteenth and early four-teenth centuries have concordances external to the motet repertoire, in independent song or refrain contexts (listed in Table 5.1). Eight of these concordances are with complete songs, of which seven are preserved in the text-only chansonnier **Douce 308**.[14] **Douce 308** is collection of song texts organised by genre, which is thought to have been copied in Metz around 1310 and does not carry any author attributions.[15] Just three song tenors – one in **Mo** 7 (HE DAME JOLI) and two *grand chant* tenors in **Tu**, discussed later – have more than a single surviving complete concordance beyond the motet repertoire. And only one song tenor has an extant song concordance that is *not* in **Douce 308**: **Mo** 7's NUS N'IERT JA JOLIS, an anonymous and unnotated rondeau in **PaB**. Song-tenor concordances are therefore scarce and their external survivals are prevailingly anonymous, such that the only vernacular-texted tenor for which there is any evidence of authorship is the rondeau refrain HE RESVEILLE TOI associated with Adam de la Halle.[16] Why, one might ask, are there so few song concord-ances, let alone attributions, for vernacular tenors? And why are external survivals almost always, and solely, in **Douce 308**?

---

13 Beyond **Mo** and **Tu**, motets on song tenors are rare in Continental sources (see also n. 39): **Ba** records three of them and **Reg** preserves two. **Bes** groups four of the song-tenor texts in its table of contents (as nos. 29–32) and – as if the scribe were unfamiliar with this motet type – lists their tenor text incipits, rather than those of the motetus, as is usual. On the basis of the concordance patterns, I presume that the CIS A CUI JE SUI tenor listed as **Bes**, no. 29 probably indicated the motet on this tenor corresponding to **Mo** 7, no. 280, rather than to **Mo** 7, no. 272.

14 Four of these songs in **Douce 308** are located in the section devoted to ballettes, one is with the pastourelles, and two – both in **Tu** motets absent from **Mo** – are *grands chants*.

15 On the date of **Douce 308**, see Stones 2013–14, vol. 2, part 1, 41–53.

16 Although the **Tu** tenor QUANT LA SAISONS DESIREE appears as one of several lyric interpolations in a text attributed to Girart d'Amiens, this cannot reflect the authorship of the song. Girart's text is dated c.1285 (see Saly 1981), but the (unattributed) song *Quant la saisons desiree* is already extant in **Trouv. U**, in a section of the source copied by the 1250s; see Tyssens 2015.

Song Tenors and the Ballettes of Douce 308: An Unwritten Repertoire?

That songs quoted in motet tenors should have had such a seemingly limited dissemination is initially counter-intuitive. In fact, it suggests that motet composers chose as their tenors precisely the kinds of well-known and relatively popular songs whose transmission and circulation – unlike the typically higher-register *grands chants* of the sort amply preserved in trouvère anthologies – did not rely on written records. The circumstances of such songs would be comparable with those of the polyphonic rondeau, which (as demonstrated in Chapter 1) were often quoted, but had a very slight manuscript survival vis-à-vis the well-preserved motet repertoire. **Douce 308** is an atypical and largely unique witness to otherwise undocumented and lower-register songs that are included here among the group labelled 'pastourelles' (which has one of the five concordances for **Mo** song-tenor motets) and, especially, in a section devoted to nearly two hundred texts under the heading 'ballettes' (with four complete concordances for **Mo** tenors).

Scholars such as Christopher Page, Eglal Doss-Quinby, and Samuel N. Rosenberg have puzzled over the relationship between **Douce 308**'s largely unique ballette texts – which they consider an isolated and probably local Lorraine repertoire – and 'mainstream' trouvère practices.[17] They express surprise that the obscure ballettes were apparently thoroughly and quickly absorbed into Parisian circles, and were of such formal significance for lyric practices in the fourteenth century.[18] In response, Yolanda Plumley has tentatively asked 'whether the ballettes were also known in Parisian circles soon after their composition, perhaps even before they were copied into **Douce 308**' in the early fourteenth century.[19] In fact, there is concrete evidence to accept that this was indeed the case. **Mo** fascicle 7 already preserves three motet tenors with ballette concordances, and there is an additional ballette concordance with a tenor in fascicle 5 of the old corpus. The functional role of these songs as tenors is a strong signal that they already constituted

---

17 Page 1998, 383; Doss-Quinby and Samuel Rosenberg 2006, xxiv.
18 Page 1998, 388, proposes: 'It would appear that soon after 1300, a few talented individuals in Paris, and perhaps only one, made decisive and innovative use of a song-form that had only recently come to the city, quite possibly from somewhere along the Lorraine-Champagne border.' See also Doss-Quinby and Rosenberg 2006, lxxix, on the presence of **Douce 308** ballettes in **Mo**.
19 Plumley 2013, 42. At 33–34 Plumley convincingly questions the sense of **Douce 308** as an isolated collection conveyed by Page and by Doss-Quinby and Rosenberg.

genuine quotations by the 1290s.[20] I would argue, therefore, that **Douce 308** does not represent the beginning of an isolated ballette tradition. It is rather a relatively late gathering together of song texts, apparently without an established or widespread written transmission, which had been circulating in practice beyond Lorraine for at least several decades. It is even possible that these types of songs were, unusually, included in **Douce 308** because it was planned from the outset as a text-only chansonnier. That is to say, written exemplars for ballette melodies simply did not exist in the manner in which they did for *grands chants*, thus precluding their inclusion in any chansonnier destined for musical notation.

This hypothesis is borne out not only by the circumstances of the song-tenor motets recorded in **Mo 5** and **7** but also the appearance of two refrain texts with concordances in **Douce 308** ballettes in a gathering of letters and songs preserved as part of the miscellany manuscript **Lat. 15131**.[21] A concluding booklet of fourteen folios in a single hand records a collection of Latin prose and verse, intermingling letters, some macaronic devotional poetry, sermons, and the texts of seventeen multi-stanza songs, built around Latin refrains, stated at the beginning and end of every stanza. Each song is preceded by the text of a French refrain, often followed by the indication 'contra in Latino'.[22] **Lat. 15131** can be quite precisely dated: one of its Latin verses describes a flood that occurred after the celebration of Epiphany in the year 1289.[23] And one of its letters – which are preoccupied with details of life at the Abbey school of Saint-Denis, just outside Paris, and evidently originated and were probably intended for students within this environment – refers to Pope Nicholas. It is likely that this is Nicholas IV (1288–1292), and that the letters and songs must therefore have been copied between 1289 and 1292.[24] Only four of the seventeen vernacular refrain cues in **Lat. 15131** are known in other contexts: two (vdB 117 and 1159) are

---

20 Plumley 2013, 34–42, illuminates further connections between the upper voice of motets and ballettes preserved in **Douce 308**. Some of these connections are clear quotations (see 37), while others seem more like shared lexis (see 39). I limit the discussion in this chapter to **Douce 308** ballettes with motet tenor concordances, whose quotational status in **Mo** is much more certain. Nevertheless, the more general overlap in vocabulary and theme between **Mo 7** and **8** motets and **Douce 308** ballettes confirms that parts of these repertoires are interconnected and probably contemporary.

21 See the discussion and transcriptions of **Lat. 15131** in Hauréau 1892, 264–80; Thomas 1928.

22 On the presentation and format of the Latin songs in **Lat. 15131**, see Caldwell 2018, 285–86 and 302–03.

23 The year given in the Latin poem is the 'old style' date 1288. Since the month concerned is January this equates to 1289 'new style'. For a complete transcription and discussion of the text, see Thomas 1928, 498–500.

24 See Samaran and Marichal 1974, vol. 3, 339.

in the second *Dit enté* (*Gracieus temps*) by Jehan de Lescurel in **Fauv**, and two are among the ballettes of **Douce 308** (vdB 1420, which is also found as a refrain in *Renart le nouvel*, and vdB 1476).[25]

The complete texts of the two ballettes in **Douce 308** match precisely the syllable count and rhyme schemes of the corresponding Latin devotional songs in **Lat. 15131**.[26] It is telling that these two ballettes, exclusively preserved in **Douce 308**, were sufficiently known in the early 1290s at the Abbey of Saint-Denis that their melodies, and the structure of their texts, were taken up as the basis of Latin devotional songs. Moreover, simply the texts of the ballette refrains sufficed to cue their corresponding melodies. This testifies fairly conclusively to the unnotated existence and circulation of a least some of the **Douce 308** ballettes in and around Paris, at least as early as the 1290s. It is worth noting too that the proportion of unique vernacular refrains (thirteen out of seventeen) in **Lat. 15131** is very high. The melodies to which these Latin songs were to be sung, melodies evidently familiar enough to be cued merely by a refrain text or incipit, were not therefore of the kind usually preserved for posterity.

Interconnected traces of a tradition of largely unwritten, 'popular', vernacular songs are principally confined to a small set of sources, and are found in varied but quite particular contexts. The song tenors in **Mo** 7; the unusually large body of around seventy (mostly notated) refrains interpolated in Jacquemart Gielee's *Renart le nouvel*; and the refrain cues in **Lat. 15131** are all preserved in manuscripts dated – quite definitely in the latter two cases – to the early 1290s.[27] Additional traces in the first decade of the fourteenth century, among the ballettes of **Douce 308** and the incomplete author corpus of Jehan de Lescurel appended to **Fauv**, testify to the endurance of these melodies for at least two decades. The lack of evidence for an extensive or continuous written tradition does not deny their circulation in oral practice. All of the manuscript contexts outlined earlier constitute

---

25 The text concordance for vdB 355 in *Le livre d'amouretes* noted by Anne Ibos-Augé is doubtful since only two of the four refrain words in **Lat. 15131** match *Le livre d'amouretes* precisely. See her *REFRAIN: Musique, poésie, citation: le refrain au moyen âge/Music, Poetry, Citation: The Medieval Refrain* (accessed 10 September 2020), http://refrain.ac.uk/view/abstract_item/355.html.

26 As noted in Doss-Quinby and Rosenberg 2006, 358, the Latin text accompanying vdB 1420 in **Lat. 15131**, *Nicolai sollempnio*, corresponds exactly to the form of ballette no. 125 in **Douce 308**. *Marie preconia*, whose refrain cue is vdB 1476, also matches exactly the form of ballette 33 in **Douce 308**.

27 Butterfield 1998, 112–20, provides a useful overview of the tradition of interpolated refrains before **Fauv**; of connections between Adam de la Halle, *Renart le nouvel*, and **Douce 308**; and of the complex and flexible circulation of refrains within different copies of *Renart le nouvel* itself.

special cases or circumstances that apparently motivated the commitment to writing (without musical notation in **Lat. 15131** and **Douce 308**) of a typically more informal vernacular song milieu.[28]

Song Tenors and the Ballettes of Douce 308: Attribution and Authorship

The principal source of evidence for such songs, the chansonnier **Douce 308**, unfortunately does not include any composer attributions, even for the many of its *grands chants* that are typically preserved elsewhere as part of author compilations (and with their melodies). Doss-Quinby and Rosenberg endorsed Maria Carla Battelli's hypothesis that there was a brief period around the turn of the thirteenth century into the fourteenth when song compilations abandoned authorship as their organising principle in favour of genre.[29] They posited that 'as collections became further removed chronologically from the period of composition of the songs they transmitted, and attributions were lost, a song's paternity became less pertinent or significant than its adherence to generic categories'.[30] Yet it is difficult to accept that absence of authorship is evidence of its absence, certainly in the case of those very well-known *grands chants* in **Douce 308** consistently attributed elsewhere to major trouvères. Such *grands chants* include those by Gace Brule or Thibaut de Champagne, who had had, for quite some time, an already historical status in the context of their mid- or late thirteenth-century authorial collections. It is hard to see how an extra decade or two should make a substantive difference to the relevance of Gace Brule if his identity had already endured for more than half a century after his death.

Arguably, then, generic organisation need not necessarily reduce (or reflect the reduced importance of) authorial connotations, and it is perhaps understandable that a collection of texts as sizeable as **Douce 308** might dispense with the additional demand of including attributions. The more pressing question, however, concerns the significance of author identity beyond

---

28 Earp 1991, 102–03, views the repertoire of 'dance lyrics' (102) in **Douce 308** as part of an oral and even improvised tradition. He suggests that the fundamental flexibility and ephemerality of this repertoire was the reason for its 'scanty transmission' (103). Although some of these melodies probably were flexible, others had a sufficiently fixed identities to assume the function of motet tenor quotations, or to serve as identifiable tunes for Latin devotional contrafacta in **Lat. 15131**. Flexibility and ephemerality alone, therefore, cannot account for the lack of extant written evidence.

29 See Battelli 1999; Doss-Quinby and Rosenberg 2006, lix–lx. As demonstrated in Lug 2012, organisation by genre is not an exclusively late thirteenth-century feature and may be particular to the Lorraine region.

30 Doss-Quinby and Rosenberg 2006, lx.

the written 'mainstream' of the high-style *grand chant*. That is, did concepts of authorship prevail within what may have been a more informal but arguably more genuinely mainstream oral tradition of songs of the kind adopted as motet tenors and recorded in writing within the ballette texts of **Douce 308**?

Not only the paucity but the anonymity of extant evidence for this song tradition makes the importance of authorship very difficult to adjudicate: **Mo**'s song tenors are mostly known only in this anonymous motet collection, and **Douce 308**'s ballettes are also confined to a manuscript that does not include attributions. The concordance for the **Mo** 7 tenor NUS N'IERT JA JOLIS as a polyphonic rondeau in **PaB** is also anonymous, but so are the four rondeaux in this source elsewhere ascribed to Adam de la Halle (see Chapter 1). The outward conventions of such a tiny number of surviving manuscripts cannot be used to argue the case one way or the other. This notwithstanding, it must be considered that the repertoire of short, formally flexible, and heavily refrain-dependent songs used as tenors in **Mo** might not invoke or belong to a single identifiable poet and/or composer in the same way as a *grand chant*.

The authoriality of the refrain is relevant here, since it is clear that these short phrases of poetry and music circulated widely and freely, in works by different authors, and with adaptations to their texts and/or melodies. Once again, modern-day scholars are not in a position to know the authorship of individual refrains or the connotations of authorship that certain refrains may have carried: this is not the kind of information that is ever made explicit in surviving sources. The survival of evidence to link the tripartite refrain text and melody of the HE RESVELLE TOI tenor to Adam de la Halle is exceptional. Exceptional too are the links perceptible between refrain melodies by or associated with Adam and interpolations in *Renart le nouvel* (especially the copy of this romance in **Ha**, the manuscript that also contains Adam's author corpus). Nevertheless, it seems highly unlikely that all or even most refrains would have been definitively tied to an author's identity. Some or indeed many were sufficiently generic and ubiquitous that they must have assumed the status of proverbial and conventional poetic and musical vocabulary. Refrains, rather than complete songs, were used for just three vernacular-texted tenors in **Mo** 7: CIS A CUI – for which a full ballette text survives in **Douce 308** – was subjected to six repetitions as the tenor of no. 272 and stood at the head of a different tenor, a cento of nine individual refrains, in no. 280;[31] and the slightly more extended refrain melody QUI PRENDROIT was repeated three times as the tenor of three different motets (**Mo** 5, no. 175; **Mo** 7, no. 277; and **Mo** 7, no. 302). In these cases, claims of authorship seem dubious, yet the comparable **Mo** 8 tenor FRESE NOUVELE – comprising four repetitions of a Parisian

---

31 On this cento tenor, see Thomson 2017, 143–48.

street cry – could plausibly have invoked the distinctive advertising style of a particular market stall or seller.

Song-Tenor Forms and Characteristics

Characteristics of the song tenors in **Mo** testify to a high degree of formal flexibility and mixing, as well as to a relatively formulaic musical style that could place them in a similar category to refrains as regards authorship. The fixed song forms of the late thirteenth and early fourteenth centuries are, as demonstrated by Page, fundamentally interrelated.[32] The tripartite *pedes cum cauda* form (aab or ab ab x) of many *grands chants* becomes a ballade with the addition of a final refrain. Add to this an initial refrain and the ballade becomes a refrain-framed virelai, such that these forms – as especially evident among the ballettes of **Douce 308** – are intertwined and sometimes interchangeable within what Page terms a 'ballade-virelai matrix'.[33] Rondeaux, by contrast, stand out for their exclusive use of the musical material of a two-part refrain (A and B) and for partial internal recapitulations of their refrain text and music, but they share the feature of a framing refrain with virelais.

Five song-tenor motets (three in **Mo** 7, one in fascicle 8, and one in **Tu**) have a conventional rondeau form (AB aA ab AB) whose accompanying textual repetitions are in three cases corroborated by surviving poetry (see Table 5.1).[34] Three motets (two in fascicle 7 and one in fascicle 8) have the typical overall AbbaA form of a conventional virelai, for which surviving text concordances for the fascicle 7 pieces confirm the presence of a framing refrain.[35] Three further pieces in fascicle 8 have a simpler AbA virelai form, in which new material is apparently sandwiched between a refrain. One tenor in **Mo** 7, the extended BELE YSABELOS (no. 256), is a genuine hybrid, which – like a virelai – includes material (here labelled c) unrelated to its framing refrain as

---

32 Page 1998, 369–74.

33 In the two versions of the same *pedes cum cauda* form song tenor D'UN JOLI DART in **Mo** 8 (nos. 309 and 321) the first is like a virelai, since it includes the refrain at the outset as well as the conclusion, while the second omits the initial refrain, giving the appearance of ballade form (see Table 5.1). This latter version, with only the concluding refrain, is the form of the text among the pastourelles of **Douce 308**.

34 The motet tenor NE ME BLASMES MIE of **Mo** 8, no. 318, has an alternative rondeau form that presents the refrain's B (rather than A) material in its second couplet.

35 Copied twice among **Douce 308**'s ballettes (nos. 36 and 112). Doss-Quinby and Rosenberg 2006, lxxxi; Plumley 2013, 30–31 considered the tenor JE LA TRUIS TROP ASPRETE to be a rondeau, despite its overall AbbaA form and, crucially, the presence of non-refrain material. Nevertheless, I do not deny the proximity to the rondeau of the eight-line AB cc ab AB form of the three tenors in **Mo** 7 and 8 that I classify here as virelais. JE LA TRUIS TROP ASPRETE highlights the fundamental crossover between ballette, rondeau, and virelai forms.

well as the internal recapitulation of the refrain text and melody typical of a rondeau, although here of the refrain's B (rather than A) material.

In general, though, strictly conventional rondeau and virelai tenors prevail in fascicle 7, which would seem to represent the earliest extant layer of motets on song tenors, while the song tenors of fascicle 8 and **Tu** are more varied. Alongside **Mo** 8's three simple virelai-like AbA tenors, there is a trend towards slightly longer and loftier tenor forms entirely absent from fascicle 7: the twice-used fascicle 8 tenor with the refrain '*D'un joli dart*', which has a concordance with the pastourelle *Defors Compeigne* in **Douce 308**, is in the larger-scale *pedes cum cauda* form. **Tu** preserves three motets with rondeau tenors, including one not found in **Mo** 7 or 8, but two of the **Tu** motets absent from **Mo** have *grand chant* tenors, both with concordances in **Douce 308**, in *pedes cum cauda* form (see Table 5.1). The final vernacular texted tenor in **Mo** 8, LONC TANS, quotes a widely transmitted motetus voice, rather than a song, a phenomenon apparent too in the **Tu** unicum that quotes the **Mo** 7 motetus (also recorded earlier in **Tu** itself) *Lis ne glai*.

This formal and registral shift, towards *pedes cum cauda* form, *grand chant*, and motetus tenors in fascicle 8 and **Tu**, results in a notable increase in the survival of concordances: all of these tenors are found beyond **Douce 308**, and their melodies consistently survive in contexts external to the motets in question. Both of the *grand chant* tenors in **Tu** are recorded in additional chansonniers, and with melodies. In the case of *Quant la saisons desiree*, these chansonniers (**Trouv. O**, **Trouv. U**, and **Trouv. V**) do not typically carry attributions. **Trouv. R**, however, which records the text and melody of the tenor ORENDROIT PLUS, does normally include rubrics with author attributions, but not in the case of this particular song. Once again, sample numbers are simply too small to draw definite conclusions, but this lack of attribution in the context of a *grand chant*, and where it could have been possible, warns against the assumption that song tenors necessarily carried connotations of authorship.

The rather generic nature of repetitive song-tenor melodies likewise undermines their distinct identity in every case. The opening gesture of the JE LA TRUIS TROP ASPRETE virelai was, as noted earlier (see Example 5.1), something of a stock figure among instrumental tenors. Among song tenors, the prevalence of leaps of a fifth (and often from D to a) is a common thread. The virelais tenors RIENS NE VOUS VAUT (unique to **Mo** 8, no. 333) and HE DAME JOLIE (**Mo** 7, no. 290 with concordances in **Douce 308** and **CgC 11**, whose syllable counts and rhyme scheme perfectly complement the musical form of the **Mo** 7 tenor), both begin their non-refrain (c) material in this same way. Similarly, the hybrid rondeau-virelai tenor BELE YSA-BELOS begins its new c material a fifth higher than that of its refrain. In the fascicle 8 tenor NON VEUL MARI (**Mo** 8, no. 323, a simpler AbA or ab cc ab virelai), every single phrase begins with the opening D – a leap of a fifth.[36] In the virelai-like (unlabelled) tenor of the unique **Ivrea** motet *Clap, clap/ Sus Robin*, the internal non-refrain material (which itself is in *pedes cum cauda* form) is likewise caracterised by an opening D – a leap (see the final row of Table 5.1). Another distinctive feature similarly typical of virelai tenors is an insistence on repeated pitches at the beginning of phrases.[37]

These musical tendencies among virelai-form motet tenors offer significant clues as to the likely melodic profile of some of **Douce 308**'s largely lost and often virelai-form ballettes. In this regard, it is also worth noting that five song tenors – four with ballette concordances in **Douce 308** – have paired initial phrases, in which the opening material is immediately repeated, leading to a different (closed) musical cadence.[38] Thanks to the notated survival of song-tenor motets, and principally those in **Mo**, one may hypothesise that ballette melodies were often characterised by repetitive and repeated-note, paired refrain phrases, and new, non-refrain material that was frequently pitched a fifth higher in tessitura and/or included leaps of a fifth.

As to the circumstances determining the choice of song quotations as motet tenors, one might reasonably and cautiously conclude that these were diverse. Register may have played a role in the perception of authorship, but it would be simplistic to equate 'popularity', or flexible and/or oral transmission, straightforwardly with anonymity. As discussed in Chapter 1, the opening rondeau of Adam de la Halle's *Jeu de Robin et Marion, Robin m'aime*, varies across its surviving written sources, particularly as regards the extent and poetic content of the material framed by its refrain, itself probably quoted rather than newly created by Adam. Though evidently circulating orally and in a number of versions, this rondeau (which is not strictly conventional in its form in any of the extant versions) and indeed its (quoted) refrain were very likely still associated with Adam's identity. Some of the songs adopted as tenors may well have been linked to particular author or performer personalities, while others may not. As in the case of refrains, some songs may have had very fixed and distinctive melodies while others may have circulated in several different musical versions – perhaps encouraged by their mixed and fundamentally flexible forms – or had their texts attached to a number of different established melodies. Again similarly to

---

36 Leaps of a fifth (D – a) also predominate in the motetus voice *Lonc tens*, transposed down an octave and adopted as a tenor in **Mo 8**, no. 337.

37 These are the tenors of **Mo 7**, no. 295 and **Mo 8**, nos. 313, 325, and 333. **Mo 7**, no. 295 has a concordance with a ballette in **Douce 308**. The initiation of phrases with repeated pitches also characterises the alternative virelai and ballade forms of the versions of the same tenor in **Mo 8** nos. 309 and 321, with a pastourelle concordance in **Douce 308**.

38 These are the tenors of **Mo 5**, no. 164; **Mo 7**, no. 727; **Mo 7**, no. 290; **Mo 7**, no. 295; and **Mo 8**, no. 333. Only the tenor of **Mo 8**, no. 333 does not have a ballette concordance in **Douce 308**.

the situation of refrains, some of the songs may have had an exclusive or pronounced local circulation (as has conventionally been presumed for the majority of ballettes in **Douce 308**) while others may have had widespread and even international currency.

French Song-Tenor Motets in English Sources

This last suggestion is supported by a consideration of the nine extant motets in English sources from the late thirteenth and early fourteenth centuries that employ French-texted tenors (see Table 5.2). These song tenors exhibit both significant similarities and differences to those in **Mo** and **Tu**. Although no single tenor is shared between the two repertoires, there is clear evidence of exchange between the French and Anglo-Norman milieux. The **Mo** 7 tenor HE DAME JOLIE survives as a ballette text in **CgC 11**, and the text of its refrain is also quoted in an early fourteenth-century Anglo-Norman love letter (**CgC 54**). Moreover, a complete concordance for a Continental song-tenor motet, *Au cuer, ai un mal/Ja ne m'en repentirai/JOLIETEMENT*, survives in the English manuscript **Douce 139**.[39] Such French–English connections are further corroborated by fact that the song tenor of the English motet *Ade finit perpete/Ade finit misere/A DEFINEMENT D'ESTE LERRAY* is concordant with an otherwise unique pastourelle in **Douce 308**. Only one other of the nine French-texted song tenors in English manuscripts has an external (text) concordance, and this is a refrain among the fourteenth-century collection of *fatras* attributed to Watriquet de Couvin in **Fr. 14968**.[40]

In spite of these connections, the French-texted tenors in English manuscripts exhibit consistent differences, both in their selection and treatment, from their Continental counterparts. Four out of nine of these tenors are relatively similar to the newly composed 'pes' foundations characteristic of English motets: they involve repetitions of a single phrase, probably a refrain, a procedure in the minority amongst Continental song-tenor motets. These refrains share, in two instances, the standard paired phrase structure – the a and b material varying only in its open or closed cadences – common also in the refrain tenors of French motets. However, of the remaining tenors only one – the virelai tenor MARIOUNETTE DOUCHE – is identifiable

---

39 French sources with complete concordances of song motets are limited to **Mo**, **Ba**, **Bes**, **Reg**, and **Tu**. On **Douce 139**, see Everist 2007, 371 n. 20. The only further concordance for a song-tenor motet, in **Wilh**, is partial. The complete music and text of the Latin motetus (*Imperatrix supernorum*) of **Mo** 7, no. 272 occupies the recto of the front flyleaf of a twelfth-century copy of St Bernard's sermons on the Song of Songs from the Cistercian nunnery of Wilhering, with the rubric 'mutetum de beata virgine'.

40 See Dillon 2012, 139–40.

Table 5.2 Thirteenth- and early fourteenth-century motets in English sources with French-texted song or refrain tenors

Song tenor (order follows Harrison 1980)	Motet concordances (* indicates tenor texted in full)	Song or refrain concordances (attributions indicated in bold, where known; **Douce 308** = text only)	Musical form	Observations
A DEFINEMENT D'ESTE LERRAY	**Onc** (fol. 87v) **Tours** (fol. 166r)	**Douce 308** Pastourelle (RS 436)	ab b'c b'c'	3 statements of overall abb form
MARIOUNETTE DOUCHE	**Onc** (fol. 89r) (= Tenor melody, here retexted *Virgo mater*, of *Caligo/ Virgo\Contra\Tenor* **Onc**, fol. 88v)	—	a bb a a	Conventional virelai
TROP EST FOL	**Add 24198*** (fol. 1v) **Onc*** (fol. 85v) (Tenor is split between two voices, which alternate texted and untexted passages)	—	aa bb aa aa bb + closing hocket	?Voice-exchange repetitions of a refrain. b material begins with 5th leap (D – a). Repeated note phrase openings
DOUCEMENT MI RECONFORT	**Ob 7*** (fols. 267r – 268r)	Refrain (vdB 618) of a fatras by Watriquet de Couvin (**Fr. 14968**, text only)	3 × through-composed melody	?Repetition of through-composed melody

HEY HURE LURE	**DRc 20*** (fol. 1r)	—	3 × aab	?Repetition of a refrain. b shares a opening, leading to different cadence
EN AI JE BIEN TROUVE	**Tours** (fol. 1v)	—	6 × ab	?Repetition of a refrain. b shares a opening, leading to different cadence
SI J'AVOIE A PLAINGANT	**Tours** (fols. 1r and 165r) (Contratenor on fol. 165r)	—	aa' b	?Complete song melody
OR SUS ALOUETE	**Tours** (fols. 166r and IIr) (Continuation of song text in margin?)	—	abb c c	Overall abb form
VA DORENLOT	**Tours** (fol. IIr)	—	7 × a	?Repetition of a refrain

with a standard, fixed song form, while the remaining tenors are largely idiosyncratic or apparently through composed. This stands in contrast to the prevalence of virelai and especially rondeau tenors in **Mo** and **Tu**. The leaps of a fifth and the insistence on repeated notes at the beginning of phrases characteristic of motet tenors in French sources are evident in only a single English motet tenor, TROP EST FOL. Although the sample size is small, the choice and treatment of French tenors in English motets nevertheless reflects an apparently local taste for what was desirable in a polyphonic foundation, as well as a local availability of or preferences for particular song materials – perhaps predominantly stand-alone refrains or phrases – and song forms that differed somewhat from those on the Continent.

Conclusions

The significant presence within **Mo** 7 and 8 of motets based on quotations that were not drawn from liturgical plainchant melodies represents something of a conceptual shift in the context of motet authorship. Whatever the rich contextual associations of plainchant quotations as motet tenors, any strong sense of an author for these long-established chant melodies or (usually biblically derived) texts cannot have been in play. The quotation of instrumental melodies or vernacular songs as motet tenors is a different case. The identity of tenor performers or composers is made explicit in **Mo** 7 in the melodies whose labels name Tassin and Loyset. Moreover, the majority of song (musical and poetic) quotations chosen as motet tenors were much more likely to have been created within living musical memory – and their creators still in living memory – than were chant quotations. Although song-tenor texts are laboriously provided in full for the cluster of three such motets in **Ba**, **Mo** gives a complete vernacular text only for the refrain-cento CIS A CUI tenor (**Mo** 7, no. 280). **Tu** preserves this same cento text in its entirety, as well as the texts of its two *grand chant* tenors.[41] Otherwise, only the opening words of the mostly rondeau and virelai tenors are given in **Mo** and **Tu**: these songs were apparently current and well known enough that knowledge of their texts could be taken for granted. There is no written trace of a culture of attribution for such types of songs, but it is undeniable that the prevalence of composer-performers and concerns of identity played a more significant role in such secular musical and poetic cultures than in liturgical ones.

---

41 This is not simply a matter of *mise-en-page*: in **Tu**, the two fully texted *grand chant* tenors (of motet nos. 15 and 17) surround the motet (no. 16) on the rondeau-virelai hybrid BELE YSABELOS, only the beginning of whose text is provided.

Remarkably, song tenors in **Mo** are, in fact, treated with greater respect for their musical and formal integrity than their chant counterparts. While plainchant melismas are – as was long conventional – excerpted from their broader musical context and subjected to artificial rhythmic patterns and repetitions, French motets based on songs quote these songs in their entirety. Crucially, and unlike the treatment of instrumental melodies attributed to Tassin and Loyset or of individual refrains, songs are stated only once in motet tenors, which thereby preserve undisturbed their original rondeau, virelai, and *pedes cum cauda* forms. That the form of these songs was evidently of some importance is confirmed, as Mark Everist has demonstrated, by the fact that such underlying tenor structures are frequently reflected in the upper voices of motets.[42] Again in contrast to plainchant tenors, and as emphasised at the outset, not only the original formal characteristics but also the original rhythm of refrain and song tenors was maintained in their new polyphonic contexts. The secular melodies selected as motet foundations were, therefore, treated in a much less abstract way than liturgical ones. This could testify to a kind of lived experience of and familiarity with such music, and as part of a predominantly oral culture, which made unpalatable – or even impossible – any disengagement of melodic, rhythmic, and formal elements of the kind established for plainchant melismas.

Of course, certain liturgical chants had geographical and local resonances thanks to their associations with particular saints or devotional practices. And these melodies were known, sung, and indeed created by the same musicians who sang and made motets. Petrus de Cruce was, after all, paid to compose a rhymed Office for St Louis. Yet contemporary plainchants of this sort were almost never adopted as motet tenors, even in the late thirteenth century, when earlier liturgical traditions and conventions dictating the selection of plainchant tenor segments were often breeched.[43] Song, as opposed to plainchant, tenors, then, probably carried more deeply embedded implications of musical personalities in the contemporary contexts of their polyphonic elaboration. The anonymity of written records of motets and their song tenors notwithstanding, questions of creative identity and ownership now pertained to all voices of a song-tenor motet in a new way, and late thirteenth-century motets on secular tenors, therefore, marked a shift in the nature of both motet composition and authorship.

---

42 See Everist 2007.

43 I know of only one motet tenor drawn from a rhymed Office composed in the thirteenth century: DECANTATUR, from the *Gaudeat Hungaria* Office for Saint Elizabeth of Hungary. See Bradley 2017.

Conclusions

The preceding chapters have investigated several, occasionally overlapping, types of late thirteenth-century motets – those by and quoting Adam, those by Petrus, those that name musicians, and motets based on secular instrumental or vernacular tenors – all of which first appear prominently, and sometimes uniquely, in fascicle 7 of the Montpellier codex. This raises questions as to the nature of **Mo** 7 itself: whether its compilers deliberately aimed to collect these particular types of pieces, or whether they simply sought to add to the codex's earlier fascicles as many new available motets as possible. **Mo** as a whole is the most substantial surviving witness to thirteenth-century motet compositions. Its final fascicles, and fascicle 8 in particular, preserve a layer of the repertoire that is not always well represented in other sources. Apart from the earlier manuscript **Ba** (a substantial repository of one hundred motets) and the later booklet of thirty-one motets in **Tu** (bound into an otherwise non-musical miscellany manuscript), most of **Mo** 7's concordances are in sources whose survival is partial or fragmentary: the table of contents for the lost motet collection **Bes**, the single remaining bifolios in **Reg** and **Leuven**, an ad hoc musical addition among documents and charters in the English manuscript **Douce 139**, or the lone motetus voice in **Wilh**, copied onto the flyleaf of a manuscript from the Cistercian nunnery of Wilhering in Austria. These latter two sources are proof that, even if external witnesses are now modest, the **Mo** 7 repertoire travelled beyond France. The significance of **Mo**'s testimony, particularly to the later thirteenth-century motet repertoire, may therefore have more to do with its size and its very survival than any conscious curation of interrelated compositions on the part of its compilers.

Apart from the opening pair of pieces by Petrus, the organisation of fascicle 7 appears somewhat impromptu: motets by Adam are not grouped, nor are pieces quoting him. Motets on song tenors are dispersed across the fascicle, as are those which use heavily syllabic semibreve tripla, despite the fact that clustering such respective pieces could have enabled a more consistent

DOI: 10.4324/9781003259282-7

mise-en-page. One has the sense that works were added as another exemplar came to hand: the run of six Latin double motets (nos. 282–87) in the middle of the fascicle for instance, or the exceptional series of three (out of a total of seven, otherwise dispersed) unica in the fascicle's main body (nos. 276–78). The start of the first of these three motets was, unfortunately, copied on **Mo** 7's missing bifolio, but its tenor is – unusually and uniquely for a thirteenth-century motet tenor – drawn from the sequence melody *Ave verum corpus*. The tenor arranges the first eighteen notes of sequence in two different rhythmic patterns, the first of which features a regular period of extended silence (three perfect long rests) that on three occasions is matched in the motetus, such that – in stark contrast to the typical relentless three-voice texture of a thirteenth-century motet – the triplum declares a string of syllabic semibreve pairs unaccompanied. This unusual unicum is followed by a pair of motets described by Mary E. Wolinski as 'daring' in their use of the sixth imperfect mode (with tenor ordines of three breves followed by a breve rest), the first also characterised by intricate three-voice hockets at the breve and semibreve level.[1] It seems, therefore, that the scribe of **Mo** 7 copied these three experimental motets, otherwise unknown and perhaps the work of a single composer, from a common exemplar before turning back to more conventional and widely disseminated fare.

The layered complexion of fascicle 7 is most evident in its two supplements, each copied by a new scribe. The first supplement records eight works that are otherwise lost to posterity – such that the unica here number more than the seven in the fascicle's entire main body of thirty-eight motets – and, as discussed in Chapter 4, it may have been the work of a northern scribe or reproduced from exemplars with Picard orthography. The music scribe's notational habits are different: in contrast to the main body of the fascicle, dots of division are used in the first supplement to clarify chains of semibreve pairs, and four semibreves within the time of a perfect breve seems to be the accepted maximum in this repertoire, which also includes three of fascicle 7's five motets on instrumental tenors. Unlike the first supplement, which involved the provision of two new gatherings, the second looks more like a filling in of leftover space. The three compositions added to the end of **Mo** 7 (nos. 300–03) are eclectic but their choice was not, it seems, entirely random. The first is a Latin double motet, often considered to be English (and similar to no. 275 in the fascicle's main body); the second is a two-voice Latin composition attributed to Philip, the erudite Chancellor of Notre-Dame of Paris, who died in 1236; and the third is a motet on the same song tenor as no. 277 and whose motetus includes a quotation of

---

1   See Wolinski 2018, 191–92 at 191.

one of Adam's rondeau refrains (also quoted in no. 291).[2] The most puzzling choice here is the two-voice motet *Laqueus conteritur/LAQUEUS*, also included within an opening fascicle devoted to Latin songs and motets by Philip in **LoB**, a manuscript dated in the 1260s.[3] Philip's old-fashioned motet is the only two-voice work preserved in **Mo**'s final fascicles and required considerable readjustment of the prepared page layout. Gaps in stave rulings to produce the two-column format intended for the fascicle's separate motetus and tripum voices were here filled in, quite clumsily, to allow the continuous notation of the lone motetus voice.

Might the scribe of **Mo** 7's second supplement have gone to such trouble to record *Laqueus conteritur/LAQUEUS* because this motet was known to be by Philip? Like Adam, Philip received a dedicated author corpus, and one which also – though exclusively Latin-texted – included both monophonic and polyphonic works. Again like Adam, Philip's posthumous reputation was long-lived, and his texts enjoyed a large-scale revival in the early fourteenth-century manuscript **Fauv**. The Chancellor's two-voice motet was antiquated at the time when **Mo** 7 was copied, and he could hardly have had any personal contact with composers of Adam's or Petrus's generation. Rather, an appreciation of Philip as part of a more distant, elevated musical heritage, and a realisation that he was not represented elsewhere in **Mo**, could have prompted the unexpected and visually disruptive inclusion of *Laqueus conteritur/LAQUEUS* as the penultimate motet in fascicle 7.[4] That fascicle 7 was, in consequence, framed by compositions from Petrus de Cruce at its opening and a much older, two-voice motet by Philip the Chancellor near its close may have been a deliberate gesture.

Since so few attributions are known or knowable for thirteenth-century motets, there is always a danger that music historians and analysts may place too much interpretative weight on the scant traces of authorship that remain. At the same time, however, this book has demonstrated that connections which might initially be dismissible as too small or simply coincidental – a single word ('Aucun' or 'Entre') or a short musical phrase – often reward closer investigation. The picture assembled here from multiple examples and often apparently minor details has revealed not only new quotations – such as

---

2   On English motets in **Mo** 7 and 8, see Everist 2018, 21–24. For Philip's biographical details, see Thomas B. Payne, 'Philip the Chancellor', *Grove Music Online* (accessed 25 Aug. 2020), https://doi.org/10.1093/gmo/9781561592630.article.21561.

3   *Laqueus conteritur/LAQUEUS* appears in **LoB** on fol. 43r. On the date of **LoB**, see Payne 2011, xxxi. See also Whitcomb 2000; Deeming 2015.

4   Fascicle 6 of **Mo** is devoted to two-voice French motets but the old corpus does not have a collection of two-voice Latin pieces. The supplement to **Mo** fascicle 3, apparently added at the same time as fascicle 7, also preserves two two-voice Latin motets, as well as two two-voice French pieces. Two of these pieces are unica but the other two have concordances in **F**.

Petrus's opening quotation of Adam in *Aucun ont trouve* or the direct modelling of the text of *Entre Jehan et Philippet* on *Entre Adam et Haniket* – but also new meanings in previously identified ones. These include the deliberate positioning of Adam as old-fashioned in the *Se je sui* triplum that quotes his 'Chief bien seans' incipit, for example, or the significance of the syllabic-semibreve tripla assembled in the patchwork *Par une matinee* triplum in fascicle 8, which is headed by the quotation of an old-corpus motet that pre-empts Petrus's division of the perfect breve into four. There are surely more quotations to find and to understand among the repertoire of fascicle 7, as well as nuances that will never be recoverable.

Through the analysis of surviving compositions, it has been possible to establish that Adam was widely quoted in late thirteenth-century motets, of which one is known to be by Petrus. This invites further speculation, both about Adam's influence as well as his relationship with Petrus. Although, as stressed in Chapter 1, Adam's motets appear quite conventional if not a little conservative in the context of **Mo** 7, they nonetheless exhibit several features that persisted in the subsequent development of the genre. In the case of *Aucun se sont/A Dieu commant/SUPER TE*, Adam's use of a new tenor melody from a responsory outside the conventional body of plainchant sources for motets or for polyphony in the earlier *Magnus liber* is typical of a growing trend across **Mo** 7 and 8. In **Mo** 7, the established mid-century motet tenors – APTATUR, OMNES, and PORTARE – are still strongly in evidence. But they feature here alongside new types of plainchant foundations – notably Mass Ordinary chants (Kyrie and Ite Missa est) and Marian antiphons – that typically had not previously been treated in polyphony. The tenors of Petrus's two known compositions (ANNUNTIANTES and ECCE IAM) are unique amongst motets and apparently newly chosen by him, but unlike Adam's SUPER TE, there is proof that both host chants received earlier organum settings.[5] Adam, seeking to replicate in a motet tenor the harmonic foundation of his three-voice polyphonic rondeau, was actually more radical than Petrus in his free selection of the SUPER TE melisma, unconstrained by any polyphonic heritage or convention. It is Adam's practice of plainchant tenor selection that is characteristic of later, fourteenth-century motets, where tenors are rarely reused and typically drawn from an unlimited range of plainchant sources to meet

---

5 ANNUNTIANTES is from the Gradual *Omnes. Surge et illuminare* [M 9], but – unconventionally – from the respond of this gradual, which was not included in extant polyphonic organum settings of this chant in the *Magnus liber*. ECCE IAM is part of the *Alleluia. Ecce Iam* [M 82] for which a two-voice organum survives in **StV**. Apart from SUPER TE, the only other new/unique tenor in **Mo** 7 from an Alleluia, Gradual, or Responsory for which no organa survive is SURREXIT [M 75], the tenor of no. 298.

musical and/or poetic requirements particular to the composition at hand, rather than from an established stock of quotations or host melodies.

In the context of later fourteenth-century developments, Adam's multi-sectional motet *De ma dame vient/Dieus, comment porroie/OMNES* seems similarly prophetic. As emphasised in Chapter 1, this motet is unique in the thirteenth-century repertoire because it uses two different established versions of the OMNES plainchant melisma. Adam creates an unusually intricate large-scale structure by treating his OMNES tenor(s) to a total of three different rhythmic arrangements, each repeated four times, and with refrain quotations appearing at structural junctures (the end or beginning of a new pattern). The use of varied tenor rhythmicisations features in six further motet tenors in **Mo** 7, and notably in both of Petrus's known motets (although he uses just two different patterns rather than three).[6] A tendency towards clearly sectionalised motets, as well as to effect change in a tenor's rhythmic pattern between sections, is fundamental to many later fourteenth-century works. This technique cannot be credited as Adam's invention, but the form and scale of *De ma dame/Dieus, comment/OMNES* and Adam's decision to vary his tenor melody as well as rhythm stand out in the context of **Mo** 7.[7]

The choice, melody, and arrangement of the OMNES tenor to accompany the **Mo** 8 triplum *Se je sui* (no. 316, discussed in Chapter 1), which concludes with a quotation of Adam's 'Chief bien seans' incipit may, therefore, be significant. OMNES, the only tenor used twice among the motets ascribed to Adam, is an unusually old-fashioned tenor by the standards of **Mo** 8. The creator of *Se je sui/Jolietement/OMNES* employed the nine-note version of the melisma exploited by Adam in *De ma dame/Dieus, comment/OMNES* but much less common than the ten-note version, also used by Adam in this same composition and in most other late thirteenth-century motets. As in Adam's motet, the **Mo** 8 motet presents the OMNES melisma in three different rhythmisications, all of which (save the initial statement) open with an unusual and rhythmically disorientating breve rest at the beginning of the modal foot.[8] The triplum *Se je sui* explicitly positioned its text and its unrelenting syllabic semibreve declamation as more expressive than Adam's 'Chief bien seans'. It seems that the choice of the OMNES tenor to accompany this **Mo** 8 triplum, its melodic version, and rhythmic arrangement represented a further reference to a second motet by Adam. Once again, the invocation of Adam was intended as an unfavourable comparison: to point up the novelty of *Se je sui/Jolietement/OMNES*

---

6   These are **Mo** 7, nos. 253, 254, 276, 277, 289, and 296. Nos. 253, 254, and 276 have only two different rhythmic patterns, but all others use three, usually proceeding from slow to fast.

7   On the use of different rhythmic tenor patterns in earlier motets, see Bradley 2017, 680–82.

8   See the discussion in Wolinski 2018, 193.

and to emphasise its tenor rhythmicisation as much more adventurous than in Adam's *De ma dame/Dieus, comment/OMNES*. That the composer of *Se je sui* like Petrus in the incipit of *Aucun ont trouve*, positioned Adam as representative of an old style that they were improving is proof of a complex reception for Adam's works. Whatever the perspective or purpose of later motet creators, that they felt the need to react to Adam's motets confirms rather than denies his influence and legacy.

Such interpretations and claims for Adam's importance are necessarily hypothetical. But the techniques emphasised earlier – freer tenor selection and multi-sectional compositions – are part of a changing landscape in late thirteenth-century motet composition, characterised by new and different priorities and a greater range of possibilities. Adam was undeniably participating in, if not influencing and actively instigating, a more pronounced interpenetration between song and motet cultures, and one that crucially involved polyphonic as well as monophonic songs. In the late thirteenth century, both motets and polyphonic rondeaux were three-voice genres. Motets on song tenors are closer to polyphonic rondeaux in the relative rhythmic equality of their three voices – though here with the song melody at the bottom rather than in the middle of the texture – than to motets in the rhythmically stratified, syllabic semibreve style. These two new motet types in the late thirteenth century move in essentially opposite directions, but both prioritise song in different ways. While some motets adopt the melodies and rhythms of pre-existing songs as their musical foundations, those with declamatory tripla favour much slower or even unpatterned plainchant tenors in order to support a rapid, expressive, and soloistic presentation of a vernacular text in their highest voices. It is striking that contrafacta survive for none of these kinds of motets in fascicle 7.[9] The prevalent earlier thirteenth-century habit of making new texts for old music was, apparently, no longer desirable or even viable in motets based either on song tenors or with declamatory tripla.[10]

It is not that practices of reuse or recomposition disappear altogether in the late thirteenth century, but rather that they take different forms. As discussed in Chapter 4, there is a new tendency to create wholly new

9 The single exception is a relatively early example of a syllabic triplum motet which has an extant contrafactum text. In the copy of *Quant vient en mai/Ne sai que je die/IOHANNE* in **Leuven**, the Latin contrafacta *Divini roris* and *Arida frondescit* (also cited by Franco) are copied directly underneath the French texts.

10 In several late thirteenth- or early fourteenth-century motets the practice of providing new music for old texts so prevalent in **Fauv** is evident. For instance, **Mo 8**, no. 326 – which quotes an older Latin conductus text (extant in **F**) in its motetus – or the appearance of the upper-voice texts of **Mo 7**, no. 275 in **Onc** in a different musical setting.

tripla – in both text and music – for existing three-voice works, and to use pre-existing two-voice foundations as well as more predictable and regular motetus voices (in both Latin and French) as the basis for declamatory semibreve vernacular tripla. Such tripla can accommodate much lengthier (and, in consequence, loftier) texts than are typical of earlier thirteenth-century motets, and in these poetic pretensions they seem closer to fourteenth-century motets, where the voices are similarly rhythmically stratified and which, as noted earlier, are often multi-sectional works based on a wide range of plainchant tenors. Although the degree and intensity of semibreve declamation associated with Petrus did not endure in motets of the fourteenth century, what did endure was a more fixed and exclusive relationship between music and poetry evident in such late thirteenth-century tripla as well as in song-tenor motets.

Late thirteenth-century motets apparently enjoyed greater fixity, perhaps even a more work-like status, which goes hand in hand with the increased visibility of their author figures and their interest in describing musical communities. In this respect, the compositions of **Mo**'s final fascicles feel closer to fourteenth-century 'works' by Philippe de Vitry and Guillaume de Machaut than to early thirteenth-century motets, either short and heavily refrain-dependent vernacular compositions or Latin motets based on clausulae. Late thirteenth-century motets on vernacular song quotations can – as Mark Everist has suggested – be seen as the ancestors of the fourteenth-century interest in polyphonic *formes fixes*: Continental song-tenor motets are almost exclusively French-texted in all voices, and their upper voices often mirror the underlying forms of their tenors.[11] This could explain the move away from the quotation of refrain melodies, and the demise of short vernacular refrain quotations more generally, in the fourteenth century. Vernacular refrains in the fourteenth century were largely confined to polyphonic songs, rather than motets, in which the formal role and significance of the refrain precluded the casual quotation of brief musical and poetic mottos or the thirteenth-century tendency to quote several refrains within a single voice. Fourteenth-century motets, by contrast, with texts in both Latin and French, are closer to late thirteenth-century pieces in the stratified and declamatory-triplum style. Such thirteenth-century tripla themselves do not quote refrains – in the sense of short, self-contained musical and poetic

---

11 See Everist 2007. Only three out of 27 extant Continental motets on vernacular tenors feature a Latin-texted voice: the motetus of **Mo** 7, no. 272; the triplum of **Mo** 7, no. 302; and the motetus of **Mo** 8, no. 309. In the latter, a Latin motetus supports a patchwork of syllabic triplum quotations, opening with *Par une matinee*. It is possible that **Mo** 8, no. 309's use of a Latin motetus was inspired by the first motet quoted in its triplum: *Par une matinee/ Mellis stilla/DOMINO*.

phrases – but rather are party to shared poetic lexis and themes, often reflections on song-making.

In certain respects, types of late thirteenth-century motets recorded in **Mo** 7 might appear transitional, a compositional flash-in-the-pan or ultimately even something of a dead end. It is hard to think of many subsequent compositions as strange and extravagant as Petrus's *Aucun ont trouve*, for example, and the practice of making motets – with multiple independent texts in musical voices – on top of song tenors was also apparently short-lived. I have attempted here to draw out continuities in compositional technique with subsequent fourteenth-century practice even if in their surface appearance such compositions are quite different. The reputations of Adam de la Halle and Petrus de Cruce undoubtedly lived on well into the fourteenth century. Was Adam, revered in lyric poetry, somewhat scorned by later polyphonists, including Petrus?[12] But was Petrus, to a certain extent, less influential than Adam, his multi-semibreve tripla principally theoretical curiosities? This book has opened up such questions through close readings of surviving, and mostly anonymous, motets themselves. It has sought to reveal ways in which thirteenth-century motet creators engaged with the musical personalities and compositional techniques of Adam and Petrus, situating such engagement as part of an increased awareness of and preoccupation with the authorship and identities of musicians – singers, instrumentalists, and composers – towards the end of the thirteenth century.

---

12 On Adam's 'pivotal role . . . in the history of lyrical writing' as depicted in the *Dit de la panthere*, see Huot 1987a, 193–208 at 202.

Bibliography

Anderson, Gordon A. 1969. 'Newly Identified Clausula-Motets in the Las Huelgas Manuscript'. *Musical Quarterly* 55, 228–45.

Aubry, Pierre. 1907. *Recherches sur les tenors français dans les motets du treizième siècle*. Paris.

Baltzer, Rebecca A. 2018. 'The Decoration of Montpellier 8: Its Place in the Continuum of Parisian Manuscript Illumination'. In Bradley and Desmond, eds. 2018, 78–89.

Bartsch, Karl, ed. 1870. *Romances et pastourelles françaises du XIIe et XIIIe siècles*. Leipzig.

Bastin, Julia. 1942. 'Review of Gilbert Mayer, *Lexique des oeuvres d'Adam de la Halle* (1940)'. *Romania* 67, 383–97.

Battelli, Maria Carla. 1999. 'Le antologie poetiche in antico-francese'. *Critica del testo* 2, 140–89.

Bent, Margaret. 2015. *Magister Jacobus de Ispania, Author of the* Speculum musicae. Royal Musical Association Monographs 28. Farnham.

Berger, Roger, ed. 1963–70. *Le Nécrologe de la Confrérie des jongleurs et des bourgeois d'Arras, 1194–1361*. 2 vols. Mémoires de la Commission Départementale des Monuments Historiques du Pas-de-Calais 11/2 and 13/2. Arras.

———, ed. 1981. *Littérature et société arrageoises au XIIIème siècle. Les chansons et dits artésiens*. Arras.

Besseler, Heinrich. 1927. 'Studien zur Musik des Mittelalters. II. Die Motette von Franko von Köln bis Philipp von Vitry'. *Archiv für Musikwissenschaft* 8, 137–258.

Billen, Claire. 2014–15. 'Quand les jongleurs dissent la fraude fiscal (Arras XIIIe siècle)'. *Baetica: Estudios de Arte, Geografía e Historia* 36–37, 73–88.

Blume, Clemens and Henry Marriot Bannister, eds. 1905. *Tropi Graduales. Tropen des Missale im Mittelalter: Tropen zum ordinarium Missae*. Analecta hymnica medii aevi 47. Leipzig.

Bradley, Catherine A. 2017. 'Song and Quotation in Two-voice Motets for Saint Elisabeth of Hungary'. *Speculum* 92, 661–91.

———. 2019. 'Choosing a Thirteenth-Century Motet Tenor: From the *Magnus liber organi* to Adam de la Halle'. *Journal of the American Musicological Society* 72, 431–92.

———. 2020. 'Review of Jennifer Saltzstein, ed., *Musical Culture in the World of Adam de la Halle*'. *Revue de musicologie* 106, 491–94.

Bradley, Catherine A., and Karen Desmond, eds. 2018. *The Montpellier Codex: The Final Fascicle: Contents, Contexts, Chronologies*. Woodbridge.

———. 2018b. 'Introduction'. In Bradley and Desmond, eds. 2018, 1–10.

Branner, Robert. 1977. *Manuscript Painting in Paris During the Reign of Saint Louis: A Study of Styles*. Berkeley, Los Angeles, and London.

Butterfield, Ardis. 1991. 'Repetition and Variation in the Thirteenth-Century Refrain'. *Journal of the Royal Musical Association* 116, 1–23.

———. 1998. 'The Refrain and the Transformation of Genre in the *Roman de Fauvel*'. In *Fauvel Studies: Allegory, Chronicle and Image in Paris, Bibliothèque nationale de France, MS français 146*, eds. Margaret Bent and Andrew Wathey, 105–60. Oxford.

———. 2002. *Poetry and Music in Medieval France: From Jean Renart to Guillaume de Machaut*. Cambridge.

———. 2011. 'Vernacular Music and Poetry'. In *The Cambridge Companion to Medieval Music*, ed. Mark Everist, 205–24. Cambridge.

Caldwell, Mary Channen. 2018. 'Cueing Refrains in the Medieval Conductus'. *Journal of the Royal Musical Association* 143, 273–324.

Catalunya, David. 2017. 'Nuns, Polyphony, and a Liégeois Cantor: New Light on the Las Huelgas "Solmization Song"'. *Journal of the Alamire Foundation* 9, 89–134.

———. 2018. 'Insights into the Chronology and Reception of Philippe de Vitry's Ars Nova Theory: Revisiting the Mensural Treatise of Barcelona Cathedral'. *Early Music* 46, 417–38.

Corbellari, Alain. 2019. 'Adam de la Halle: Cleric and Busker'. In Saltzstein, ed. 2019, 231–48.

Crocker, Richard. 1990. 'French Polyphony of the Thirteenth Century'. In *The New Oxford History of Music*, 2: *The Early Middle Ages to 1300*, eds. David Hiley and Richard Crocker, 636–78. 2nd edn. New York and Oxford.

Cruse, Mark, Gabriella Parussa, and Isabelle Ragnard. 2004. 'The Aix "Jeu de Robin et Marion": Image, Text Music'. *Studies in Iconography* 25, 1–46.

Curran, Sean. 2013. 'Vernacular Book Production, Vernacular Polyphony, and the Motets of the "La Clayette" Manuscript (Paris, Bibliothèque nationale de France, Nouvelles acquisitions françaises 13521)'. Ph.D. diss., University of California, Berkeley.

———. 2018. 'A Palaeographical Analysis of the Verbal Text in Montpellier 8: Problems, Implications, Opportunities'. In Bradley and Desmond, eds. 2018, 32–65.

Deeming, Helen. 2015. 'Preserving and Recycling: Functional Multiplicity and Shifting Priorities in the Compilation and Continued Use of London, British Library, Egerton 274'. In *Manuscripts and Medieval Song: Inscription, Performance, Context*, eds. Helen Deeming and Elizabeth Eva Leach, 141–62. Cambridge.

Desmond, Karen. 2018a. 'Texture, Rhythm, and Stylistic Groupings in Montpellier 8 Motets'. In Bradley and Desmond, eds. 2018, 139–60.

———. 2018b. *Music and the moderni 1300–1530: The ars nova in Theory and Practice.* Cambridge.

———. 2018c. 'Semibreve Notation in England and the "Late" Ars Antiqua'. Unpublished Paper Given at *Ars Antiqua III: Music and Culture in Europe c1150 to c1330.* Lucca.

Diergarten, Felix. 2014. '"Vient a Point Ton Bordon": Art Song Reworking im Codex Ivrea'. *Basler Jahrbuch für historische Musikpraxis* 38, 137–54.

Dillon, Emma. 2012. *The Sense of Sound: Musical Meaning in France, 1260–1330.* The New Cultural History of Music. New York and Oxford.

Doss-Quinby, Elgal, and Samuel Rosenberg. 2006, with Elizabeth Aubrey. *The Old French Ballette: Oxford, Bodleian Library, MS Douce 308.* Publications Romanes et françaises 239. Geneva.

Earp, Lawrence. 1991. 'Lyrics for Reading and Lyrics for Singing in Late Medieval France: The Development of the Dance Lyric from Adam de la Halle to Guillaume de Machaut'. In *The Union of Words and Music in Medieval Poetry*, eds. Rebecca A. Baltzer, Thomas Cable, and James I. Wimsatt, 101–31. Austin.

Everist, Mark. 1989. *Polyphonic Music in Thirteenth-Century France: Aspects of Sources and Distribution. Outstanding Dissertations in Music from British Universities.* New York and London.

———. 1996. 'The Polyphonic *Rondeau* c. 1300: Repertory and Context'. *Early Music History* 15, 59–96.

———. 2007. 'Motets, French Tenors and the Polyphonic Chanson ca. 1300'. *Journal of Musicology* 24, 365–406.

———. 2018. 'Montpellier 8: Anatomy of. . .'. In Bradley and Desmond, eds. 2018, 13–31.

———. 2019. 'Friends and Foals: The Polyphonic Music of Adam de la Halle'. In Saltzstein, ed. 2019, 311–51.

Ferreira, Manuel Pedro. 1998. 'Mesure et temporalité; vers L'*Ars nova*'. In *La Rationalization du temps au XIIIe siècle: musique et mentalités*, Actes du colloque Royaument 1991, ed. Catherine Homo-Lechner, 65–120. Grâne.

Gallo, F. Alberto. 1970. 'Motetti del primo trecento in un messale di Biella (codice Lowe)'. In *L'Ars Nova Italiana del Trecento III*, ed. F. Alberto Gallo, 215–45. Certaldo.

———. 1985 (1977). *Music of the Middle Ages II*, trans. Karen Eales. Cambridge. First published as *Il Medieoveo II.* Turin.

Garnier, Jacques. 1859. *Dénombrement du temporel de l'évêché d'Amiens en 1301.* Amiens.

Gennrich, Friedrich. 1957. *Bibliographie der ältesten französischen und lateinischen Motetten.* Summa musicae medii aevi 2. Darmstadt.

Géraud, Hercule. 1837. *Paris sous Philippe-le-Bel: D'après des documents originaux.* Paris.

Gómez, María Carmen. 1985. 'Une Version a Cinq Voix du Motet "Apollinis Eclipsatur/Zodiacum Signis" dans le Manuscrit "E-BCEN" 853'. *Musica Disciplina* 39, 5–44.

Goudesenne, Jean-François. 2000. 'L'Office de s. Winoc de Bergues (Flandres, XIe siècle) est-il à l'origine d'une teneur dans les motets du XIIIe siècle? Recherches sur la teneur *Aptatur* dans les motets des manuscrits de Montpellier et de Bamberg'. In *The Di Martinelli Music Collection (KULeuven, University Archives): Musical Life in Collegiate Churches in the Low Countries and Europe: Chant and Polyphony,* Yearbook of the Alamire Foundation 4, eds. Bruno Bouckaert and Eugeen Schreurs, 283–95. Leuven.

Grau, Anna Kathryn. 2019. 'The *Pastourelle* and the *Jeu de Robin et Marion*'. In Saltzstein, ed. 2019, 282–301.

Grier, James. 2021. *Musical Notation in the West.* Cambridge.

Guy, Henri. 1898. *Essai sur la vie et les oeuvres littéraires du trouvère Adan de la Halle.* Paris.

Haines, John. 2010. *Satire in the Songs of Renart le Nouvel.* Geneva.

———. 2019. 'Aristocratic Patronage and the Cosmopolitan Vernacular Songbook: The *Chansonnier du Roi* (*M-trouv.*) and the French Mediterranean'. In Saltzstein, ed. 2019, 95–120.

Harrison, Frank L., ed. 1980. *Motets of English Provenance.* Polyphonic Music of the Fourteenth Century 15. Monaco.

Hauréau, Barthélémy. 1892. *Notices et extraits de quelques manuscrits latins de la Bibliothèque nationale.* Volume 4. Paris.

Huck, Oliver. 2018. 'Double Motet Layouts in the Montpellier Codex and Contemporaneous *Libri motetorum*'. In Bradley and Desmond, eds. 2018, 90–99.

Huot, Sylvia. 1987a. *From Song to Book: The Poetics of Writing in Old French Lyric and Lyrical Narrative Poetry.* Ithaca.

———. 1987b. 'Transformations of the Lyric Voice in the Songs, Motets and Plays of Adam de la Halle'. *Romanic Review* 78, 148–64.

———. 1997. *Allegorical Play in the Old French Motet: The Sacred and Profane in Thirteenth-Century Polyphony.* Stanford.

Ibos-Augé, Anne. 2018a. ' . . . *Que ne dit "cief bien seans"*': Quoting Motets in Montpellier 8'. In Bradley and Desmond, eds. 2018, 211–30.

———. 2018b. 'Adam de la Halle et les "jeux": Les premiers exemples de théâtre profane chanté à Arras à la fin du XIIIe siècle'. In *Les Villes au Moyen Âge en Europe occidentale: Ou comment demain peut apprendre d'hier,* ed. Marie-Françoise Alamiche, 229–63. Paris.

———. 2019. 'Refrain Quotations in Adam's *Rondeaux*, Motets and Plays'. In Saltzstein, ed. 2019, 249–82.

Johnson, Glenn Pierr. 1991. 'Aspects of Late Medieval Music at the Cathedral of Amiens'. Ph.D. diss., Yale University.

Jordan, William Chester. 1979. *Louis IX and the Challenge of the Crusade: A Study in Rulership.* Princeton.

Kügle, Karl. 1997a. *The Manuscript Ivrea, Biblioteca capitolare 115: Studies in the Transmission and Composition of Ars Nova Polyphony.* Musicological Studies 69. Ottawa.

———. 1997b. 'A Newly-Discovered Ars Antiqua Fragment in Leuven'. *Yearbook of the Alamire Foundation* 2, 104–19.

———. 2019. *Manuscript Ivrea, Biblioteca capitolare 115: Introductory Study and Facsimile Edition.* Ars nova 5. Lucca.

Langlois, Ernest. 1904. 'Quelques oeuvres de Richard de Fournival'. *Bibliothèque de l'école des chartes* 65, 101–15.

Leach, Elizabeth Eva. 2011. 'A Concordance for an Early Fourteenth-Century Motet: *Exaudi melodiam/Alme Deus/TENOR* Revisited'. Available at https://eeleach.files.wordpress.com/2011/08/dijon-motet2.pdf.

———. 2015. 'A Courtly Compilation: The Douce Chansonnier'. In *Manuscripts and Medieval Song: Inscription, Performance, Context*, eds. Helen Deeming and Elizabeth Eva Leach, 221–46. Cambridge.

Lefferts, Peter Martin. 1986. *The Motet in England in the Fourteenth Century*. Ann Arbor.

Ludwig, Friedrich. 1978. *Repertorium organorum recentioris et motetorum vetustissimi stili. Band I. Catalogue raisonné der Quellen. Abteilung 2. Handschriften in Mensural-Notation*. Musicological Studies 26, ed. Luther Dittmer. Brooklyn, New York, and Hildesheim.

Lug, Robert. 2012. 'Politique et littérature à Metz autour de la guerre des Amis (1231–1234): Le témoignage du Chansonnier de Saint-Germain-des-Prés'. In *Lettres, musique et société en Lorraine médiévale*, eds. Mireille Chazan and Nancy Freeman Regalado, 451–83. Geneva.

Maschke, Eva M. 2018. '*Deus in adiutorium* Revisited: Sources and Contexts'. In Bradley and Desmond, eds. 2018, 100–20.

Mason, Joseph W. 2021. '*Trouver et partir*: The Meaning of Structure in the Old French *jeu-parti*'. *Early Music History* 40, 1–45.

Maw, David. 2004. '"Trespasser Mesure": Meter in Machaut's Polyphonic Songs'. *Journal of Musicology* 21, 46–126.

———. 2006. 'Accent and Metre in Later Old French Verse: The Case of the Polyphonic Rondel'. *Medium Aevum* 75, 46–83.

———. 2018. '*Je le temoin en mon chant*: The Art of Diminution in the Petronian Triplum'. In Bradley and Desmond, eds. 2018, 161–83.

———. 2020. 'Review of Karen Desmond, *Music and the moderni, 1300–1350: The ars nova in Theory and Practice*'. *Revue de musicologie* 106, 494–501.

McGee, Timothy J. 1990. *Medieval Instrumental Dances*. Bloomington.

Mews, Constant J., John N. Crossley, Catherine Jeffreys, Leigh McKinnon, and Carol J. Williams, eds. and trans. 2011. *Johannes de Grocheio. Ars musice*. TEAMS Varia. Kalamazoo.

O'Sullivan, Daniel E. 2019. 'The Northern *Jeu-Parti*'. In Saltzstein, ed. 2019, 153–88.

Paden, William D., ed. and trans. 1987. *The Medieval Pastourelle*. 2 vols. New York.

Page, Christopher. 1993. *Discarding Images: Reflections on Music and Culture in Medieval France*. Oxford.

———. 1998. 'Tradition and Innovation in BN fr. 146: The Background to the Ballades'. In *Fauvel Studies: Allegory, Chronicle, Music, and Image in Paris, Bibliothèque nationale de France, MS français 146*, eds. Margaret Bent and Andrew Wathey, 353–94. Oxford.

Parsoneault, Catherine Jean. 2001. 'The Montpellier Codex: Royal Influence and Musical Taste in Late Thirteenth-Century Paris'. Ph.D. diss., University of Texas at Austin.

Payne, Thomas B., ed. 2011. *Motets and Prosulas: Philip the Chancellor*. Recent Researches in the Music of the Middle Ages and Early Renaissance 41. Middleton.

Pesce, Dolores. 1997. 'Beyond Glossing: The Old Made New in *Mout me fu grief/Robin m'aime/Portare*'. In *Hearing the Motet: Essays on the Motet of the Middle Ages and the Renaissance*, ed. Dolores Pesce, 28–51. New York and Oxford.

Plumley, Yolanda. 2013. *The Art of Grafted Song: Citation and Allusion in the Age of Machaut*. Oxford.

Ragnard, Isabelle. 2019. 'The Songs of Adam de la Halle'. In Saltzstein, ed. 2019, 189–227.

Raynaud-Spanke, G. 1980. *Raynauds Bibliographie des altfranzösischen Liedes. Neubearbeitet und Ergänzt von Hans Spanke*, ed. Avner Bahat. Musicologica 1. Leiden.

Reaney, Gilbert, and André Gilles, eds. 1974. *Franconis de Colonia Ars cantus mensurabilis musicae*. Corpus scriptorum de musica 15. Rome.

Rokseth, Yvonne. 1935–39. *Polyphonies du XIIIᵉ siècle: Le manuscrit H 196 de la Faculté de Médecine de Montpellier*. 4 vols. Paris.

Rose-Steel, Tamsyn. 2011. 'French Ars nova Motets and their Manuscripts: Citational Play and Material Context'. Ph.D. diss., University of Exeter.

Saint-Cricq, Gaël, ed. 2017, with Eglal Doss-Quinby and Samuel N. Rosenberg. *Motets from the Chansonnier de Noailles*. Middleton.

———. 2019. 'Genre, Attribution and Authorship in the Thirteenth Century: Robert de Reims vs "Robert de Rains"'. *Early Music History* 38, 141–231.

Saltzstein, Jennifer. 2008. 'Refrains in the *Jeu de Robin et Marion*: History of a Citation'. In *Poetry, Knowledge, and Community in Late Medieval France*, eds. Rebecca Dixon and Finn Sinclair, 173–86. Cambridge.

———. 2012. 'Cleric-Trouvères and the Jeux-Partis of Medieval Arras'. *Viator* 43, 147–64.

———. 2013. *The Refrain and the Rise of the Vernacular in Medieval French Poetry*. Cambridge.

———, ed. 2019. *Musical Culture in the World of Adam de la Halle*. Brill's Companions to the Musical Culture of Medieval and Early Modern Europe. Leiden and Boston.

———. 2019a. 'Introduction'. In Saltzstein, ed. 2019, 1–14.

———. 2019b. 'Adam de la Halle's Fourteenth-Century Musical and Poetic Legacies'. In Saltzstein, ed. 2019, 352–63.

Saly, Antoinette. 1972. 'Li Commens d'Amours de Richard de Fournival (?)'. *Travaux de linguistique et de littérature* 10, 21–55.

———. 1981. 'Les destinaires du roman de Meliacin'. *Travaux de linguistique et de littérature* 19, 7–16.

Samaran, Charles, and Robert Marichal. 1974. *Catalogue des manuscrits en écriture latine portant des indications de date, de lieu ou de copiste*. 7 vols. Paris.

Shagrir, Iris. 2019. *The Parable of the Three Rings and the Idea of Religious Toleration in European Culture*. Cham.

Small, Carola. 1993. 'Artois in the Late Thirteenth Century: A Region Discovering Its Identity'. *Historical Reflections/Réflexions historiques* 19, 189–207.

Stakel, Susan, and Joel C. Relihan. 1985. *The Montpellier Codex, Part IV: Texts and Translations*. Recent Researches in the Music of the Middle Ages and Early Renaissance 8. Madison.

Stenzl, Jürg. 1970. 'Eine unbekannte Sanctus-Motette vom Ende des 13. Jahrhunderts'. *Acta Musicologica* 42, 128–38.

Stones, Alison. 2013–14. *Gothic Manuscripts 1260–1320. A Survey of Manuscripts Illuminated in France.* 3 vols. London.

———. 2018. 'The Style and Iconography of Montpellier folio 350r'. In Bradley and Desmond, eds. 2018, 66–77.

———. 2019. 'Another Note on fr.25566 and Its Illustrations'. In Saltzstein, ed. 2019, 77–94.

Symes, Carol. 2007. *A Common Stage: Theater and Public Life in Medieval Arras.* Ithaca.

———. 2019. 'The "School of Arras" and the Career of Adam'. In Saltzstein, ed. 2019, 21–50.

Thomas, Antoine. 1928. 'Refrains français de la fin du XIIIe siècle: Tirés des poésies latines d'un maître d'école de Saint-Denis'. In *Mélanges de linguistique et de littérature offerts à M. Alfred Jeanroy par ses élèves et ses amis,* 497–508. Paris.

Thomas, Wyndham, ed. 1985. *The Robin and Marion Motets.* 3 vols. Devon.

Thomson, Matthew. 2016. 'Interaction Between Polyphonic Motets and Monophonic Songs in the Thirteenth Century'. D.Phil. diss., University of Oxford.

———. 2017. 'Monophonic Song in Motets: Performing Quoted Material and Performing Quotation'. In *Performing Medieval Text,* eds. Ardis Butterfield, Henry Hope, and Pauline Souleau, 136–51. Cambridge.

———. 2018. 'Building a Motet around Quoted Material: Textual and Musical Structures in Motets Based on Monophonic Songs'. In *A Critical Companion to Medieval Motets,* ed. Jared C. Hartt, 243–60. Woodbridge.

Tischler, Hans, ed. 1978. *The Montpellier Codex. Parts I–III.* Recent Researches in the Music of the Middle Ages and Early Renaissance 2–7. Madison.

Tobler, Adolf, ed. 1884. *Le dis du vrai Aniel: Die Parabel von dem achten Ringe, Franzosische Dichtung des Dreizehntenjahrhunderts.* Leipzig.

Tyssens, Madeline, ed. 2015. *Le Chansonnier français U, publié d'après le manuscrit Paris, BNF, fr.20050.* Paris.

Uckelman, Sara L. 2013. 'Names in the 1292 Census of Paris'. Available at www.ellipsis.cx/~liana/names/french/1292paris.pdf.

———. 2014. 'Bynames in Medieval France'. Available at https://silo.tips/download/draft-bynames-in-medieval-france-sara-l-uckelman.

van den Boogaard, Nico H. J. 1969. *Rondeaux et refrains du XIIe siècle au début du XIVe. Collationnement, introduction et notes.* Paris.

van der Werf, Hendrik. 1989. *Integrated Directory of Organa, Clausulae, and Motets of the Thirteenth Century.* Rochester.

Walker, Thomas. 1982. 'Sui *Tenor* Francesi nei motetti del '200'. *Schede medievali: rassegna dell'officina di studi medievali* 3, 309–36.

Wegman, Rob C. 2015. 'The World According to Anonymous IV'. In *Qui musicam in se habet: Studies in Honor of Alejandro Enrique Planchart,* eds. Anna Zayaruznaya, Bonnie J. Blackburn, and Stanley Boorman, 693–730. Middleton.

Whitcomb, Pamela. 2000. 'The Manuscript London, British Library, Egerton 274: A Study of its Origin, Purpose, and Musical Repertory in Thirteenth-Century France'. Ph.D. diss., University of Texas at Austin.

Wilkins, Nigel, ed. 1967. *The Lyric Works of Adam de la Hale: Chansons, Jeuxpartis, Rondeaux, Motets.* Corpus mensurabilis musicae 44. Rome.

Wolinski, Mary E. 1988. 'The Montpellier Codex: Its Compilation, Notation and Implications for the Chronology of the Thirteenth-Century Motet'. Ph.D. diss., Brandeis University.

———. 1992. 'The Compilation of the Montpellier Codex'. *Early Music History* 11, 263–301.

———. 2008. 'Drinking Motets in Medieval Artois and Flanders'. *Yearbook of the Alamire Foundation* 6, 9–20.

———. 2018. 'How Rhythmically Innovative is Montpellier 8'. In Bradley and Desmond, eds. 2018, 184–96.

Yudkin, Jeremy. 1982. 'Notre Dame Theory: A Study of Terminology, Including a New Translation of the Music Treatise of Anonymous IV'. Ph.D. diss., Stanford University.

———. 1985. *The Music Treatise of Anonymous IV: A New Translation.* Neuhausen-Stuttgart.

Zayaruznaya, Anna. 2020. 'Old, New, and Newer Still in Book 7 of the *Speculum musicae*'. *Journal of the American Musicological Society* 73, 95–148.

Zingesser, Eliza. 2019. 'The Poets of the North: Economies of Literature and Love'. In Saltzstein, ed. 2019, 51–74.

Index of Compositions

General index

Adam de la Halle (or Adans li Boscus)
Ch. 2 *passim*, 114–21; and Arras 7,
17, 21n41, 27n46, 58n4, 59, 50–6,
63, 66, 70–1; *Congé* 50; debates
with Jehan Bretel 55; and Douai 51;
father (Henri de la Halle or Henri
Bochu, maistre) 50n19, 51n26, 55,
70n31; *grands chants* 3, 10–11; in
Italy? 50–1; *Jeu d'Adam ou de la
feuilee* 49–50, 70n30, 70n31; *Jeu
de Robin et Marion* 20–33, 26–7,
50, 53n40, 108; *jeux-partis* 7, 8n8,
49, 55, 69n28; *Le Roi de Sezile*
4, 50; life 3, 7, 49–56, 64; in **Mo**
7 and 8 Ch. 1 *passim*; in Paris?
50–1, 54, 70n30; quotations by
19–21, 27, 40n72, 53, 56n49, 118;
quotations from his works 12–13;
(of *Chief bien seans* 40–2; of *Entre
Adam et Haniket* Ch. 3 *passim*; of
Fi, mari 33–6; of the refrain *He,
Dieus, quant verrai* 36–40); quoted
in **Mo** motets 20–42, 56–7, 62–9,
118–19; reception of 40–3, 54–7,
117–21; self-quotation 6, 9, 14–20,
42–4, 53, 55n47; sources of motets
9–11
Adans li Boscus 50; *see also under*
Adam de la Halle
Amiens 49, 70, 85n33, 86–7; *see also
under* Petrus de Cruce
Anonymous IV 48, 80
Apel, Willi 76
Arras 17, 50–6, 62–3, 66, 70, 71n34;
refrains from 21n41, 27n46, 53
'Aucun. . . ' motets Ch. 2 *passim*

B. de Cluny 73
Ba 54, 82–3, 114
ballettes 86, 100n14, 101–6, 108–9
Baltzer, Rebecca A. 5
Battelli, Maria Carla 104
Bent, Margaret 2, 47, 73, 76
Berger, Roger 51–2
Bes 9–10, 54, 81n21, 82–3, 85,
100n13, 114
breve, division of *see under* notation
Butterfield, Ardis 17

Charles of Anjou 4, 50
Compiègne 87
contrafacta xiii–xvi, 47, 53n39, 63n15,
79, 82–3, 104n28, 119
Crocker, Richard 77, 79
Curran, Sean 5, 81

Dis dou vrai Aniel 4
Dit de la panthere 55, 56n48,
121n12
Doss-Quinby, Eglal 101, 104
dots of division *see under* notation
Douai 62; *see also under* Adam de la
Halle
Douce 308 86; and authorship 104–7;
song tenors in 100–9

'Entre. . . ' motets Ch. 3 *passim*
estampies 67, 89n1, 90
Everist, Mark 2, 17, 29, 58, 113, 120

Falck, Robert 17
Fastoul, Baude, *Congé* 49–51, 55,
70n88

For Product Safety Concerns and Information please contact our EU
representative GPSR@taylorandfrancis.com Taylor & Francis Verlag GmbH,
Kaufingerstraße 24, 80331 München, Germany

Printed and bound by CPI Group (UK) Ltd, Croydon, CR0 4YY
11/04/2025
01844011-0008